REGION VS NATION:

Cuyo in the Crosscurrents of Argentine National Development, 1861-1914

by

William J. Fleming

1986.

Center for Latin American Studies

ARIZONA STATE UNIVERSITY
Tempe

Library of Congress Cataloging-in-Publication Data

Fleming, William J.
    Region vs nation.

    Bibliography: p. 73
    1. Mendoza (Argentina: Province)--Economic
conditions.   2. Cuyo (Argentina)--Economic conditions.
I. Title.   II. Title: Region versus nation.
HC177.M4F55 1987   330.982'64   86-29919
ISBN 0-87918-066-8

Published in the United State of America.

With Anita

To

Jim

In Memoriam

TABLE OF CONTENTS

PREFACE

Argentina's economic growth in the late nineteenth and early twentieth centuries accelerated the rise to power and prominence of Buenos Aires city and province. Today, roughly forty percent of Argentina's population lives within the metropolitan region of the federal capital while the fortunes of the pampa's economy virtually determine national prosperity. These stark realities have mesmerized scholars for the past several decades and have caused many of them to accept the historical canon, the history of the littoral is the history of Argentina.

The rest of the country is seen as having grown or languished as a function of the coast's development. Unfortunately, research on non-pampa Argentina languished as well. Scholars concentrated on "where the action was," the pampas and littoral cities. Research that did focus on the interior often appeared as an extension of the traditional coastal orientation. Indeed, this work began more years ago than I care to recount as a Ph.D. thesis meant to reveal the discriminatory impact of foreign financed railroads and coastal development on the once vibrant and prosperous far-western province of Mendoza--"La Perla Andina" (the Andine Pearl), as it was once called.

Primary research revealed a very different story than either I had expected or than the traditional assertions of "nationalists" foretold. My understanding of the Argentine past was turned inside out as even the most certifiable assumptions about the nation's economic history seemed to be wrong. Prominent works on the building of the British railroads, for example, were so inconsistent with my early findings that I eventually discarded those works and "rebuilt" the national network from scratch by relying exclusively on primary documents, laws, resolutions, and decrees, as well as virtually unused statistical tables. The outcome bore only a marginal resemblance to the common picture that has been and continues to be painted about British railroad construction in Argentina.

Factors at work within the province had a special complication. Unlike coastal studies an economic analysis of Mendoza's past could not benefit from previous findings in related areas because none existed. There was no economic history of the province, in English or Spanish, for any era but the colonial period, and very few reliable social, political, or cultural histories. This had the advantage of freeing the research from the constraints of misleading secondary sources and the disadvantage of greatly lengthening the amount of time it took to conclude my initial research effort. It also had the "disadvantage" of revealing a provincial economy with a level of activity, a diversity of production, a complexity of commercial relations, and a vibrancy of entrepreneurial activity that were not supposed to be there.

After several more years of research, reading, and rethinking, the pieces of Mendoza's economic growth and their importance for a clearer comprehension of the nation's history began to fall into place. During those years the financial conditions of academic publishing in this country went from bad to worse and the prospects of publishing a book on non-pampa Argentina went with them. Since the mid-1970s more than a dozen young scholars from outside Argentina have conducted research projects on the interior; little of it has been published. In the meantime, specialized works on coastal topics continue to be printed. Many of them have made important contributions to our understanding of Argentina's history and such research needs to continue. But I fear that our vision of Argentina's development will remain unnecessarily blurred until we accept a different perspective than that dictated by a timeworn canon.

For these reasons I feel especially indebted to the director, editors, and staff of the Center for Latin American Studies and its monograph series at Arizona State University. Their willingness to publish a work on non-coastal Argentina is to be applauded. Their assistance in rectifying various editorial difficulties that had worked their way into the manuscript over the course of numerous revisions is very much appreciated. I apologize to the reader for the financial exigencies that resulted in our having to eliminate half of the original manuscript from the pages that follow.

It is a source of personal joy that at long last I can recognize in print the support, advice, assistance, and constructive criticism of numerous individuals and institutions without whom this work would have remained only an idea. It is also, unfortunately, a source of no little anguish that James R. Scobie, the friend, advisor, and critic in whose memory this work is dedicated, cannot receive his due acknowledgement. On both a personal and professional level I accumulated a debt of gratitude to him that death rendered unpayable. Here I can do no more than offer a public recognition of that debt while wondering at how hopelessly powerless words can be when we are so in need of their being otherwise.

Financial support for various aspects of the original research and subsequent refinements for this book came from several sources. For their generosity I wish to thank especially: Indiana University for grants from the Latin American Studies Program, the President's Council on the Humanities, the President's Council on the Social Sciences, and the Summer Faculty Fellowship Program; The Organization of American States for a dissertation year fellowship; the Faculty Research Council of Pan American University; the National Endowment for the Humanities Summer Seminars program for a grant to participate in a seminar on Latin American Economic History at the University of Chicago; and the Inter-University Consortium on Political and Social Research for a travel grant to participate in a seminar on quantitative historical analysis at the University of Michigan.

A special thanks goes to the personnel of several libraries and archives both in this country and in Argentina whose goodwill and invaluable assistance made research a joy and a success. In the United States these include the staffs of the Library of Congress, The Regenstein Library of the University of Chicago, and the Benson Collection of the Institute for Latin American Studies at the University of Texas. In Argentina these include the staffs of the: Archivo Histórico de Mendoza, Archivo del Diario Los Andes, Archivo Judicial, Archivo y Biblioteca de la H. Legislatura, Archivo de Rentas, Junta de Estudios Históricos de Mendoza, Biblioteca San Martín, Archivos de la Dirección de Irrigación, Archivo de Geodesia y Catastro, and Dirección de Investigaciones Económicas y

Tecnológicas, all in the Province of Mendoza; and the Archivo del F.C. Buenos Aires al Pacífico, Biblioteca Tornquist, Biblioteca Nacional, Biblioteca del H. Congreso, and the Instituto Geográfico Militar, all in greater Buenos Aires.

John Coatsworth and Tom Davies read different versions of the entire manuscript and offered invaluable criticisms. As a teacher as well as a scholar, John V. Lombardi's advice and direction has been fundamental to much of my career. Sometimes a conversation that helps shape ideas is as important as assistance in locating material. For fulfilling one of those roles and sometimes both, I wish to express my appreciation to the following individuals: Jorge Balán, César García Belsunce, Jonathan Brown, Germán Céspedes, Edmundo Correas, Georgette Dorn, William Glade, Paul B. Goodwin, Donna Guy, Ramona del Valle Herrera, Eduardo Herrera, Arthur Leibscher S.J., Sandra McGee, Carlos Marichal, Pedro Santos Martínez, Michael Mullaney, Robert Oppenheimer, Donald Peck, Lance Query, John L. Rector, David Rock, Richard Slatta, and Carl Solberg.

For more personal sacrifices than one should have to render, her considerable editorial skills and acute critiques, as well as her patience and understanding, I am particularly indebted to my wife, Anita. I am also grateful for the support of Grace and Lester Reid and of my parents. Finally, whatever merit lies within the pages of this work I share happily with all of those who have helped me; whatever shortcomings exist I retain as mine alone.

Chapter 1

Changing Vantage Points

On Argentine Development

The economic history of Argentina stands as an almost unshakeable and embarrassing challenge to common explanations for Latin America's economic problems. For almost all other areas scholars can point to a wide variety of factors to explain underdevelopment. Large tradition bound peasantries, persistent political instability, lopsided urbanization patterns, poor technological innovation, regressive investment activities, *latifundia-minifundia* land tenure patterns, lack of capital, and the like have all acted as causal variables in the illusive search for the historical determinants of contemporary Latin America's economic condition. This search has been made necessary by the fact that several major nations have been immersed in modern capitalist growth streams for well over 100 years without achieving sustained development.

For most countries the root causes of the growth without development syndrome seemed to lay in factors, like illiteracy and land tenure, that kept diverting the nations from the evolutionary path that led from underdevelopment to development. The path was supposedly marked out by the historical experiences of the developed countries of Western Europe and the United States. Until the 1960s and among non-marxist analysts, the notion that a linear relationship existed between underdevelopment and development went unchallenged. Since then, however, two different but related sets of principles which originated in Latin America have gained widespread acceptance and have offered strident challenges to traditional views.

The first of the three perspectives is frequently referred to as "diffusionism" because of its basic idea of how development spreads throughout the world. Put briefly, diffusionism holds that the flow of capital and technology from developed to underdeveloped nations fuels economic growth, institutional change, and sociocultural modernization and thus precipitates long-range development. For the orthodox diffusionist, if economic growth does not result in sustained development, if the "path" is diverted away from its historical destination, then the cause may be found in aberrant variables which distort or inhibit the proper functioning of the development process. In short, there is a squeaky, if not missing, gear or gears in the development machine.[1]

Unfortunately for this traditional approach, certain Latin American nations had experienced decades of rapid growth followed by repeated periods of recession if not depression that resulted in "false starts" along the road to full development. Starting in the 1960s, then, some scholars began to reexamine the relationship between Latin America and the developed nations of the world. They created in the process a direct challenge to diffusionism, dependency theory, that reconfigured the presumed fundamental relationship between underdevelopment and development.

In its initial broad brushstrokes dependency analysis seemed convincing. Underdevelopment originated not as the starting point for all economies, including those that had achieved development, but as a result of the development process itself which characterized the North Atlantic capitalist societies. A rise in demand for primary resources in the industrializing or colonial centers of the North Atlantic sent surplus capital overseas into undeveloped countries containing the needed primary resources. There, foreign capitalists and their domestic allies invested in: extracting the primary goods (from mountains, forest, farms, and ranches), building transport systems to conduct the goods to ports, port facilities to transship them, and financial institutions to capitalize the whole process. The local economy grew in response to these export sectors with the urban points of export transfer and the interior areas supplying them growing in harmony with the primary resource economy.

The diffusionist and dependency perspectives have undergone equally vigorous defenses and attacks over the last several years.[2] But these exchanges have generally failed to move us toward a more definitive understanding of Latin America's economic past. The problem lies in the fact that advocates of one view or another often rely on macro-level data equally supportive of seemingly contradictory conclusions. Indeed, diffusionism is frequently found at work only in the "center" and on the national level while dependency analysis spends much of its time in the nebulous world of international trade, capital flows, and technology transfers. In this respect the words of Frank Safford merit careful reflection: ". . . whatever one's paradigm choice, the historical analysis of underdevelopment must have as its first requirement the close study of structural realities."[3]

Within this context Argentina presents a particularly interesting case. Many of the causes cited by diffusionist studies for the growth without development syndrome never existed there while others were quickly "cured" in the late nineteenth century. Argentina, for example, never had a large tradition-bound peasantry, quickly achieved high literacy rates, underwent rapid technological change, and had ample entrepreneurial talent which manifested progressive investment tendencies. The country experienced long periods of political stability under constitutional democratic governments, had ample capital available, developed a strong economic base, and enjoyed rich resources to exploit in response to both domestic and international demand. All of the gears were in place, the machine was well-oiled with capital, the current of demand was turned on, impressive growth was generated, and underdevelopment was produced.

Viewed in general terms the historical transformations behind the growth of Argentina's economy appear to support dependency analysis. From the creation of the viceroyalty of the Río de la Plata in 1776 through Argentina's first fifty years of independence the economy grew and changed slowly. Mules, oxcarts, and cattle traversed hundreds of miles of rutted postroads and cattle trails in their arduous journeys among the provinces and between the interior and the coast. Since the colonial period commercial agriculture and stockraising had dominated the country's economy. Tallow, wool, hides, mules, steers, and related products were shipped for export over the Andes or through coastal ports. With independence, changes in international trade, and the beginning of the industrial revolution Argentina's littoral economy grew more rapidly. But persistent political instability and the relative isolation of interior-regional economies stymmied the growth of a national economy.

All of this began to change around the middle of the nineteenth century when the Battle of Pavón (1861) signaled the end of decades of political instability and led to the unification of the Argentine provinces under a single national government. The economic changes that followed were dramatic. In the mid-1800s the city of Buenos Aires had a population of roughly 90,000 while no less than 80 percent of the country's inhabitants lived in rural areas. Tucumán, the future sugar center of Argentina, in 1855 had 494 acres cultivated with cane.[4] The wheat farms and cattle ranches which would form the backbone of the national economy had yet to appear. In the 1850s Buenos Aires could not provide itself with wheat. As late as the 1870s Europe's future breadbasket imported both flour and wheat. Not until 1866 did a few cattlemen band together to propagate the benefits of fencing, quality bulls, and alfalfa pasturage for stockraising.[5]

In 1857 the country had a scant 6 miles of rail lines and an estimated 1,000,000 inhabitants, while crop farming was limited to the land immediately surrounding settlements. Thirteen years later the population had expanded to slightly under 1,900,000, the railroad "network" to 454 miles, and area sown with wheat to 321,000 acres. But within forty-five years (1870-1914), as a result of massive immigration, improved economic conditions, technological advances in agriculture and stockraising, heavy investment from abroad, and individual and governmental initiatives, Argentina found itself with 7,800,000 inhabitants, 59,300,000 acres cultivated, and nearly 21,000 miles of rails. British investment in the rail system increased from £7,600,000 in 1880 to £225,000,000 in 1914.[6] Argentina became a major exporter of beef, wheat, wool, and hides. By 1910 Buenos Aires with some 1,300,000 residents, dominated the country's foreign trade through its new deep water port facilities fed by a complex system of rail lines that radiated deep into the pampa and the interior provinces.[7]

At the core of the country's railroad network were four wide-gauge, British-owned lines: the Oeste (Western), Central, Sud (Southern), and Pacífico (Pacific). The emergence of the four lines had paralleled the development of a national economy sustained by the productive capacity of agriculture and stockraising on the humid pampa. The network was oriented toward the coast and the four wide gauge systems controlled the movement of goods and people over the pampa to and from the ports of Rosario, Buenos Aires, and Bahía Blanca as well as between the coast and the interior. The structure of this network contributed to the end of provincial insularity and the achievement of political unification. It also tended, however, to make the once vital interior economies of the north and west dependent on coastal prosperity and consumer demand.

With its comparative advantage in viticulture, Mendoza Province offered a prime example for the coastal-national view of what happened to the domestic economy of the country as a result of the building of foreign-owned railroads and the growth of exports. The Pacífico railroad headed due west from Buenos Aires to Mendoza. Once this link had been established and as the coastal population swelled, Mendoza's economy was shifted away from transandine commerce toward the provisioning of Buenos Aires province and city with wine and grapes. As a result the local economy prospered and grew only in concert with the externally dependent littoral economy and under the mercy of railroad policies and freight rates. When viewed from the provincial, interior level, however, this largely national characterization of what took place assumes a substantively distinct image.

Founded in 1561 as an outpost of the Spanish presence in South America, Mendoza remained under the administrative jurisdiction of Chile until the establishment of the viceroyalty of the Río de la Plata (1776). For political and economic reasons relations between Chile and Mendoza were not always good. In fact, between the late sixteenth and early nineteenth centuries a pattern emerged that would extend into the period of Mendoza's early modern development (1880-1914). The mendocino elite sought to either put distance between their province and Chile, or to draw closer to the latter, according to their perception of the economic future of their province within the Argentine economy.

In the seventeenth century a system of commercial agricultural trade developed that would typify Mendoza for centuries to come. As early as 1600, members of the local elite were seeking markets for wine in Córdoba, Tucumán, Buenos Aires, and Paraguay.[8] By the 1620s Mendoza was sending wine, brandy, dried fruits, local artifacts, raisins, and grapes to eastern markets. Over the Andes to Chile went wheat, flour, beef jerky, soap, and candles.[9] As more towns appeared in Argentina and as the area's existing population expanded, the importance of Mendoza's eastward commerce increased.

However, as would be the case more than two hundred years later the prosperity of Mendoza's wine trade made it an attractive target for taxation from coastal officials. By the 1660s the Cabildo of Buenos Aires was taxing wine from Mendoza and fixing its price in the local market. In 1690, the Cabildo also restricted imports of aguardiente from Mendoza to one *botija* (a large earthen jug) per oxcart. This practice led the mendocinos to lobby strongly with royal officials for the removal of all restrictions in Buenos Aires on the area's exports.

An initial declaration of free trade for Mendoza's products with Buenos Aires toward the end of the seventeenth century was reinforced in 1716 by a royal decree prohibiting any taxes, regulations, or restrictions of any kind on Mendoza's trade with

Buenos Aires except as authorized directly by the King.[10] This situation, together with the general growth of the future viceroyalty led to persistent appeals from Mendoza to be transferred out of Chile's administrative jurisdiction.

By the time the viceroyalty of the Río de la Plata was created Argentina had become the center of the southern cone's commerce. The flow of trade with Chile, which previously moved through Lima, now passed through Mendoza to and from Buenos Aires.[11] An estimated 1,000 oxcarts per year traversed the pampas between Mendoza and Buenos Aires.[12] In Mendoza the goods were transferred to mules for the week-long trek over the Andes. The carts, manufactured in Mendoza, and mules also carried a wide variety of products from Mendoza to Chile and to eastward markets, especially Buenos Aires. These exports consisted primarily of wine, brandy, flour, dried fruit, and cooking oil. After a peace agreement was signed with local Indians (1794)[13] cattleraising and the feeding of imported cattle began a sharp rise to become one of the principal industries of the province. The fattened cattle were shipped over the Andes to Chile.[14]

Although the province's economy grew during the viceregal era the mendocinos periodically complained about royal free trade policies and their effect on wine exports.[15] After the turn of the century when the movement for independence gathered support the local elite quickly sided with the revolutionaries in the hope of gaining from nationalistic economic policies that would protect local industries. Independence, however, would not bring infusions of capital, transportation improvements, or protectionist national policies.

Instead, over the next several decades the interior and coastal provinces would lock in persistent civil war over the organization of the new nation. One of the major issues in the conflicts was free trade versus protectionism. By the early 1830s the mendocinos had begun to rethink their relationships with Buenos Aires and the other coastal provinces. By this time a lively trade had developed with Chile. In violation of agreements according to which Buenos Aires was to conduct foreign policy in the name of the other provinces Mendoza negotiated its own trade treaty with Chile in 1835. At the same time, many mendocinos began to argue openly that Mendoza should leave the Argentine confederation and join the Chilean nation. This action and talk of secession brought strong protests from Buenos Aires. Local leaders responded that it is the responsibility of government to protect territorial industries. In December, 1835, a new customs law in Buenos Aires switched economic policy from free trade to protectionism. Mendoza did not leave the confederation, eastward commerce picked up, and the mendocinos developed a very profitable business in transandine cattle trading.[16]

The local economy expanded along traditional lines. Exports consisted largely of wine, flour, wheat, and dried fruit. The most significant changes occurred in the stockraising sector. By the early 1850s Mendoza had about 80,000 hectares planted with alfalfa for feed and shipped some 15,000 head of steers and 1,000 head of mules over the Andes to Chile annually.[17] Because of the slow and costly means of transportation to Buenos Aires and other eastward markets Mendoza's wine industry prospered only moderately. The transandine trade remained the most valuable for Mendoza. By 1864 the total value of imports to Mendoza equaled 600,000 gold pesos; 400,000 gold pesos from transandine imports and 200,000 gold pesos from the east. Exports equaled an estimated 830,000 gold pesos, more than half of which is represented by livestock and hides sent to Chile.[18]

Despite the hindrances of time, distance, and political instability Mendoza's eastward commerce prospered and the transandine trade expanded greatly between the 1830s and 1860s. With the achievement of national political unification in 1862 the mendocinos lobbied to acquire a rail link with their traditional coastal markets, especially Buenos Aires. The originators of the Central Argentino Railroad out of Rosario had planned to extend a branch of the line to Mendoza. They subsequently built a station at Rio Cuarto (Córdoba Province), a traditional crossroads of the mule and oxcart traffic from Mendoza. Subsequently, a separate concession was authorized by the national government in the 1870s which would eventually construct a line into Mendoza across the pampas from Buenos Aires with connections to the Central Argentino.

Although the rail link between Mendoza and eastern markets did not open until 1885, as the coastal lines extended westward Mendoza's commerce with the Argentine provinces expanded rapidly. The mendocinos had sought outlets for their wine industry in Buenos Aires and other coastal markets since the early colonial period. Once the link was achieved in the 1880s and given certain internal reforms, like the passage of a uniform irrigation law, the viticultural sector of the province's economy grew in startling proportions. What did not occur, however, was the destruction of traditional non-viticultural sectors and the reorientation of transandine trade toward the Atlantic coast.

Instead, commercial agriculture increased in response to both external and internal demand. Only wheat and flour, previously among the most important of the province's exports seemed to suffer. Provincial consumption of these two products and a switch to corn seems to have taken up much of the slack caused by the rapid expansion of wheat farming on the pampas. The trade in cattle over the Andes continued to grow throughout the 1880-1914 period despite occasional recessions and depressions. What changed in the transandine trade was the volume and composition of imports. Mendoza, as the railroad drew closer to the province, shifted to importing manufactured products and certain agricultural products not grown in the province from eastern provinces rather than from Chile or through Chilean ports and over the Andes.

In the process the province faced problems with both Chile and coastal Argentina similar to those it had experienced in the colonial and early national periods. For example, in the 1890s the prosperity of the wine industry made it a good target for taxation, from the point of view of national officials. The mendocinos fought this effort and succeeded in preventing national taxation of their wine but imposed their own tax on their most vital industry. The provincial tax increased local revenues from 1 million pesos in 1886 to 4 million pesos in 1909 and freed the province from financial dependency on the national government and the political implications that carried.[19]

In the meantime, the local government used the tax revenues to expand the infrastructure for growth and to finance lobbying efforts at the national level in defense of local interests. That defense included constant efforts to prevent the lowering of protective tariffs for the wine industry as a result of a free trade movement which became particularly strong because of the national financial crisis of the 1890s. By the turn of the century relations between Chile and Argentina became strained over a new commercial treaty. The local result was a sharp decline in cattle exports over the Andes. The Chileans offered to lower tariffs on cattle in exchange for lower Argentine tariffs on wine. Mendoza protested strongly all national tendencies to agree to the Chilean position and eventually won out.

The evolution of Mendoza's economy by 1914 had taken a path which represents a variation on established patterns. Neither the flow of foreign investments nor the structure of the transportation system such investments supported caused basic shifts in the characteristics of the local economy. Instead, export-led and foreign financed growth removed major obstacles to the expansion of the one sector of the economy that the mendocinos themselves had been trying to liberate to connect to coastal markets, especially Buenos Aires.

There is no question that national external dependency exercised a significant effect on an interior economy like Mendoza's by the eve of World War I. Provincial prosperity and revenue depended on the success of viticulture which in turn rose and fell according to the relative prosperity of consumer markets on the coast. Those markets reflected the state of the agro-export national economy.

However, to focus on this outcome as a causal explanation for what took place after 1880 ignores two sets of crucial relationships. First, this case study suggests strongly the existence of vital linkages between tradition and "modernization," and between local level analysis and our understanding of national economic growth, even when that growth is tied to international demand and capital flows. Second, with respect to those movements of capital, viewing their role in national development from the provincial level demonstrates a far more complex impact than we have imagined and explains more about the economic patterns characteristic of the pre-World War I period than do broad theories based on the results of those patterns viewed from a national-coastal or international vantage point.

Endnotes for Chapter 1

1. For a relatively recent and controversial restatement of the diffusionist view of Latin America's economic history, see: Michael Novak, "Why Latin America Is Poor," *Caribbean Review,* 11,3 (1982): 18ff.

2. D.C.M. Platt, "Dependency in Nineteenth-Century Latin America: An Historian Objects," *Latin American Research Review,* 15:1 (1980): 113-130; Stanley J. and Barbara H. Stein, "D.C.M. Platt: The Anatomy of 'Autonomy,'" *Latin American Research Review,* 15:1 (1980): 131-46; Charles Bergquist, "On Paradigms and the Pursuit of the Practical," *Latin American Research Review,* 13:2 (1978): 247-51; and Frank Safford, "On Paradigms and the Pursuit of the Practical: A Response," *Latin American Research Review,* 13:2 (1978): 252-60.

3. Frank Safford, "On Paradigms," p. 257.

4. Roberto O. Fraboschi, "Historia de la agricultura, la ganadería, y la industria," in Francisco de Aparicio and Horacio A. Difieri, eds., *La Argentina: Suma de geografía.* 9 vols. (Buenos Aires, 1959), 4:178.

5. With the formation of the Sociedad Rural Argentina (Argentine Rural Society) a few landowners sought to modernize Argentina's livestock industry. Their campaign lasted several decades, during which the society's *Anales* published articles on the latest techniques in the industry while its members led strong lobbying efforts in financial and political circles in defense of their interests. When cattle exporters in the late 1880s began paying higher prices than the saladeros (who prepared salted beef for export) for stock raised in accordance with the Sociedad's preachings, recalcitrant ranchers began rapidly to modernize their breeding methods.

6. Raymond H. Pulley, "The Railroad and Argentine National Development, 1852-1914," *The Americas,* 23 (1966-1967): 65-6.

7. James R. Scobie, *Buenos Aires: Plaza to Suburb, 1870-1910* (New York, 1974), p. 11.

8. Jorge M. Scalvini, *Historia de Mendoza* (Mendoza, 1965), p. 65.

9. Scalvini, p. 69.

10. Scalvini, p. 70.

11. Jonathan C. Brown, *A Socioeconomic History of Argentina, 1776-1860* (Cambridge, England, 1979), p. 34.

12. Pedro Santos Martínez, *Historia económica de Mendoza durante el virreinato, 1776-1810* (Madrid, Spain, 1961), p. 283.

13. Santos Martínez, *Historia económica,* p. 104.

14. Santos Martínez, pp. 94, 100.

15. Henry S. Ferns, *Britain and Argentina in the Nineteenth Century* (Oxford, England, 1960), pp. 8-9.

16. Scalvini, *Historia de Mendoza,* p. 207.

17. José L. Masini Calderón, *Mendoza hace cien años: Historia de la provincia durante la presidencia de Mitre* (Buenos Aires, 1967), p. 49.

18. Juan Llerena, "Cuadros descriptivos de las tres provincias de Cuyo," *Revista de Buenos Aires,* 11 (1866): 71-4; and Argentina, *Registro estadístico de la República Argentina* (1864), pp. 387-93.

19. Jorge Balán and Nancy Lopez, "Burguesías y gobiernos en la Argentina: La política impositiva de Tucumán y Mendoza entre 1873 y 1914," *Desarrollo Económico,* 17:67 (October-December, 1977), chart 4.

Chapter 2

The Promised Land: Mendoza During Argentina's Pre-Boom Era, 1861-1885

During the two decades that preceded the completion of railroads from Mendoza to coastal and other interior provinces the mendocinos made public policy decisions designed to stimulate long range development. Their actions resulted from the commonly held conviction that interregional exports would form the foundation for Mendoza's economic growth, and that both Rosario and Buenos Aires would provide the central markets for those products. Behind this process stood a cohesive oligarchy, interrelated by both social and family ties, which controlled provincial politics.[1] The governing elite owned ranches and farms, but they also operated stores, markets, export-import businesses, and in a few cases ventured into mining. Over time, and as a group, the ruling families had acquired a variety of entrepreneurial talents and technical skills which they utilized to improve the province's foundation for growth.

As members of the government the elite tried to modernize the economy and to provide an infrastructure for economic growth through improvements in education, transportation, and irrigation. They studied and propagated the latest techniques used in Europe, established schools of agronomy and oenology, supported an agricultural station, and reinvested their own earnings in land, seeds, plants, and equipment to increase agricultural, livestock, and wine production. In short, the elite provided the kind of exemplary economic commitment that some analysts have postulated as a requirement of growth.[2]

As a result of such efforts and of changes taking place at the national level Mendoza had developed by the mid-1880s a prosperous economy based on trade and commercial agriculture. While the transandine trade, especially in livestock, remained strong throughout this pre-railroad period, the core of the local economy "pivoted" toward the east. With changes in transportation and the initiation of pampa-based national growth local leaders sought to integrate their economy with that of the coast. The broad-based expansion of commercial agriculture in the province, however, seemed threatened by agricultural growth elsewhere in the country. By the early 1880s both private initiative and public policy began to focus strongly on Mendoza's comparative advantage in viticulture.

To some, the dangers of overemphasizing wine production and of integration into the expanding agro-export economy of the coast had already begun to appear. Nevertheless, by 1885 most mendocinos foresaw only unprecedented growth for their province once the railroad conquered the geographic isolation that had inhibited Mendoza's development in the past. Hard work, initiative, education, and supportive public policies had served the province's interests well and there seemed little reason to doubt that they would continue to do so far into the future.

The achievements of the oligarchy are evermore noteworthy given the catastrophe that struck Mendoza City in the tricentennial year of its founding. At 8:36 on the evening of 20 March 1861, the earth began to move. The mendocinos had long become accustomed to periodic tremors, but the loud rumbling noise and initial strength of this shock foretold a major earthquake. Some people recognized the signs and fled into the streets, but the suddenness, rapidity, and violence of the earthquake allowed no escape. Within seconds, the city of Mendoza lay in ruins, the graveyard of a large portion of the population.[3]

The demolished city had served as an entrepot for the oxcarts and mule trains which carried goods to and from Chile and the interior. In alfalfa fields the mendocinos fattened cattle from Córdoba, Santa Fe, and San Luis during the winter for herding across the Andes to Chile in summer. Flour mills ground wheat for export to the neighboring provinces, Córdoba, and Rosario. A small but flourishing trade existed for a number of other products, including wine, dried fruit, soap, raisins, hemp, ostrich feathers, tallow, skins, and alfalfa seed. While the rural and home industry nature of these exportable products meant that productive units located outside of the capital probably escaped damage, the earthquake had immediate and disastrous effects on Mendoza's commercial relations. Juan Llerena, who directed the province's statistical office in 1852 and the 1864 census, estimated that imports alone dropped more than 75 percent in the year following the earthquake.[4]

As for the city itself, not a single building remained standing. All dry goods stores, food markets, administrative and government offices, artisan establishments, workshops, churches, and homes, disappeared at once. In 1860, only one year before the disaster, Miguel Tristany listed 44 dry goods and food stores on just one street. Three years earlier, the Argentine Confederation census had identified 355 merchants in Mendoza City.[5] Thus, recovery meant not only restoring the flow of trade but reconstructing from rubble the commercial, industrial, and political center of the province.

On the basis of the demographic, occupational, agricultural, and livestock data reported in an extensive census taken in 1864, a fairly clear image of Mendoza's economy at this time emerges.[6] Most of the population lived in and around the capital, where irrigation facilitated agriculture, and commerce provided economic opportunities to those not directly involved in agriculture and stockbreeding. More than a third of the province's population lived in the capital and its bordering departments. Another third populated a rim of four departments to the south and southeast of this zone. The postroads over which mules and oxcarts carried goods in and out of the province passed through this central area, thus adding a further stimulus to settlement and providing additional employment through the provision of goods and services to those directly involved in trade and commerce.

All commerce, except in livestock, had to pass through the capital and its customhouse, where it was transferred from oxcarts to mules for the trip across the Andes. Those sectors involved in the cultivation, preparation, and manufacture of local goods for export, therefore, found it more convenient to locate near the center of commercial activity and transport facilities than in the more farflung districts where the soil may have been good but communications poor, and transportation of the products to the capital expensive and time consuming. These factors led to the concentration of agriculture in the core departments. There, commercial farming produced cereals, including enough wheat to supply the province's fifty flour mills, grapes and other fruit, and a large variety of vegetables. However, nearly 83 percent of the cultivated land was planted with alfalfa.

Livestock interests were similarly affected by the commercial aspects of the province's economy. Cattle, mostly from the province but also imported from San Luis, Córdoba, Santa Fe, and occasionally the province of Buenos Aires, wintered on fenced and irrigated alfalfa farms in Mendoza before crossing the Andes to Chile. Local cattle, sheep, and goats supplied meat for internal consumption, wool and hides for export, and tallow both for export and for the production of soap, large quantities of which were sent over the Andes. The livelihood of ranchers depended on a prosperous trading relationship with Chile.

Trade and commerce, given their manifest importance in Mendoza's economy, helped to generate entrepreneurial skills and experience, especially among the elite, which proved decisive for the development of the province. Because of the high percentage of native mendocinos in the population (93 percent), strong familial and social ties developed which increased elite cohesiveness and provided for a certain degree of local pride. When projected into economic activity, this spirit contributed to a unified effort to develop the province. On both an official and private level, their activities focused on irrigation, education, agriculture, transportation, and above all, the wine industry.

When it identified vast areas of cultivable land (nearly 500,000 hectares), the 1864 census commission implicitly emphasized the fundamental importance of a planned and regulated system of irrigation for economic growth. The uncoordinated distribution of water resulted in loss of harvests, shrinking productivity, and mounting litigation over water disputes.[7] Part of the problem stemmed from the absence of an irrigation law covering the entire province. Mendoza operated under guidelines set forth in the *Reglamento para el Juzgado de Aguas* (Regulations for the Water Rights Court) passed in 1844 but which only had jurisdiction over certain departments. While studies took place for a general irrigation law, the government passed a series of measures aimed at limiting the quantity of water taken from rivers, their tributaries, and canals.[8]

The overexploited Canal Zanjón, which irrigated most of the land in and around the capital, required immediate attention. In 1864, the government first tried to control use of the canal indirectly, then assumed direct responsibility for its operation and immediately appointed a commission to review applications for new taps.[9] The Tunuyán River irrigated much of the agricultural core of the province plus the stockraising areas of San Carlos and Tunuyán. Faced with steadily increasing demands on the river, the government used inspectors to assure a fair and equitable distribution of water. By 1870 the situation had become so intolerable along both the Tunuyán and Mendoza Rivers that the government placed a ban on the building of canals pending the completion of detailed capacity studies.[10]

While continuing to issue temporary measures to alleviate the most urgent problems, the authorities requested that the federal government send an engineer to Mendoza to make a general study of irrigation. The survey began in 1872 but because of a series of problems unrelated to the study itself, it apparently bore no positive results.[11] Starting in 1875 a series of commissions tried to write a general irrigation law but failed to reach a consensus before the end of the decade.[12]

An official report published in 1880 succinctly described the situation: "Each farmer tries to take maximum advantage of his land, but does not concern himself with improving it because he does not know if tomorrow he will have the water available he has today. And this is, in my judgment, the gangrene of our agriculture."[13] Farmers allowed the water they used to run off their lands uncontrolled, which resulted in the formation of small swamps and prevented its reuse. Without a systematic utilization of the Mendoza, Tunuyán, and Diamante Rivers, further agricultural development could not take place, while existing farms and ranches would suffer.

Under the auspices of the newly created post of Inspector General of Irrigation yet another census of irrigated lands was executed. It showed that the Tunuyán River irrigated 72,000 hectares in seven departments, and the Mendoza River, 42,400 hectares in six departments.[14] A total of 66 large canals tapped the Tunuyán, Mendoza, and Diamante Rivers, while 37 major streams provided additional irrigation outlets. From the large canals and streams cultivators had dug innumerable small feeder canals to conduct water to their lands.[15] The haphazard development of this labyrinth prevented the intensive and systematic exploitation of Mendoza's agricultural resources. In 1884, armed with the details provided by the census, progressive elements in the province succeeded in their longstanding attempt to pass Mendoza's first modern irrigation law.[16]

Without a rational distribution of water, new lands could not be cultivated. Without a modernized and public system of education, the new lands would not be cultivated efficiently.[17] Thus, education assumed a prominent position in the programs sponsored by every government during the period preceding the railroad. Governors commented at length on recent accomplishments, programs in progress, and remaining problems in their annual messages delivered at the opening of each legislative period. Their collective efforts included the organization of buildings, the creation and support of an agronomy school with facilities for experiments, the establishment of scholarships for needy students, and financial support for public libraries.

In 1872 the authorities approved four measures which laid the foundation for a modern education system. The first *Ley General de Educación* (General Education Law) provided for the creation of public schools in all the departments and structured their administration.[18] Governor Aristides Villanueva made primary school education compulsory and ordered the construction of a model school for advanced instruction.[19] Taking advantage of an 1870 national law which provided for agronomy schools in agricultural provinces, the government first surveyed and then ceded the land necessary for an agricultural station.[20]

Throughout the period 1872-1885 the government continued to finance the building and expansion of educational facilities, improvements in teacher training, and scholarships assigned on a school by school basis for needy students. By 1875 Mendoza had one student for every eight inhabitants, and one school for every 705 inhabitants.[21] The province had become the perennial winner of a 10,000 peso prize for high enrollment rates established in 1869 by the national government.

In an official circular sent to all municipalities in 1876 the government noted that agricultural development in the areas around Mendoza's traditional markets had led to cheaper prices and a ruinous competition. Exports from Mendoza to the coast and to towns along the way had dropped to a small fraction of their former levels. Part of the problem lay in the high cost and inefficiency of mule and oxcart transportation, difficulties which the railroad would overcome. But internally, the province needed rapid agricultural modernization. The circular recognized implicitly the impact of railroad expansion on the coast on settlement and rural output.

Unrecognized was the impartiality of a reduction in transport costs represented by railway construction. That is, all other things being equal, Mendoza faced reduced demand for some of its traditional agricultural products in coastal markets because of the development of rural zones located closer to those markets than the province was. Neither the provision of rail service for Mendoza nor internal reform could overcome such locational forces. This reality would be driven home within a few years of the railroad's completion in the mid-1880s. For the moment, however, the mendocinos continued to place strong faith in the economically liberating influence of the railroad and in the regenerative power of internal improvements.

The agronomy school consistently yielded positive results, the government claimed, but they needed to train more people faster, and to diffuse new agricultural techniques more widely and more rapidly. In pursuit of these goals the government asked the municipalities to underwrite scholarships for local students to the school. To attract students from the less developed outlying departments the government established four scholarships for students from La Paz, San Carlos, San Rafael, and Lavalle.[22] After graduation the students would return to their departments to instruct local agriculturalists in ways of improving their methods.[23]

Concern over agricultural development on the seaboard also led to a redoubled education effort in the wine industry. When a destructive fungus (oidium) attacked the province's vineyards, the officials first named a commission to study the disease and then hired an agronomist with special training in wine production. The authorities required Juan Recopet to give public lectures throughout the province on grape cultivation and winemaking techniques as well as to offer practical demonstrations in the field.[24] In 1883 the national government, at the request of local officials, sent Aaron Pavlowsky to evaluate the state of agriculture and the operations of the agronomy school in the province. He settled in Mendoza, assumed the directorship of the school, gave lectures, and wrote pamphlets on agricultural methods and the wine industry.[25] By 1884 many experiments were in progress at the agricultural station including tests with eighteen different grapestocks to determine the proper distance between plants and optimum irrigation levels.[26]

The government fostered improvements in internal transportation and actively supported construction of a rail link with the coast. Roads between and within departments were built, repaired, and improved to facilitate trade and communications. The international route to Chile through the Uspallata Pass received constant attention as did projects to build a better road through the Planchón Pass in the south. In anticipation of the extension of the Central Argentino to Mendoza, the government ordered the lengthening and straightening of the southern bypass around the capital to provide for easy access to the national postroad and the area where the railroad would enter the city.[27]

Irrigation, education, transportation: these three essential elements for the economic growth of Mendoza received constant attention from the provincial government. The measures taken in each case were designed to stimulate commercial agriculture with emphasis on alfalfa, wheat, and wine production. The first supported a lucrative cattle trade; the second, a flour export industry; and the third became the area's main economic hope. But a wide variety of other exportable agricultural products appeared consistently as candidates for minor roles in the province's development. These included nuts, fruits, vegetables, olives, corn, barley, and honey.[28]

Official stimulation of agriculture included a wide variety of major and minor projects. Lacking precise information on the size and location of cultivated lands and their crops, the government attempted repeatedly to execute property surveys. In 1867 Julio Balloffet, a French engineer living in Mendoza, received a contract to map all cultivated lands in the province starting with the core departments.[29] He failed to complete his task for technical and administrative reasons which in turn led to the reorganization of the province's topography department in 1872.[30] Subsequent surveys failed to produce more favorable results than Balloffet's efforts, however, until the turn of the century.[31]

To encourage agricultural modernization, the authorities sent exhibits and representatives to rural expositions. For example, in 1870 the legislature agreed to send two official delegates to a demonstration of agricultural machinery in Córdoba.[32] The government had already established a commission to prepare Mendoza's exhibit for the 1871 National Exposition in Córdoba. The wide variety of agricultural and pastoral products, wine, raisins, fruits and vegetables, minerals, and artisan creations in the display moved one official to call Mendoza the "promised land." He added: "Open Mendoza to the littoral through a railroad and Argentina will supply markets not only with wool and hides, but with wheat, potatoes, wine, raisins, and many, many other products."[33]

In 1873 the province arranged for a series of annual agricultural and industrial expositions of its own and began preparing for its participation in the international fair at Philadelphia. [34] For the inaugural ceremonies of the Andino extension in 1885 an official commission sponsored a major exposition of Mendoza's wealth and published a book-length account of the province's actual and potential growth.

Aware that the concentration of rural activities in the core departments left the fertile southern departments virtually unexploited, the legislature tried to induce settlement in areas around the Diamante River in San Rafael. Rufino Ortega received a fifteen-year permit in 1874 to develop and settle a large area of state property in southwestern Mendoza. According to his contract the province would grant him one square league of land (7.8 square miles) for every 1,000 pesos invested in livestock or any other rural industry; all property settled or cultivated was absolved from taxes for fifteen years; and the government would select all urban sites as well as determine the size of individual lots for colonists and the placement of streets. [35]

General provisions for colonization of the south appeared in an 1875 law that regulated the subdivision of lands, canals, streets, and urban centers. Each family of five would receive a grant of twenty square *cuadras* (1 cuadra equals 3.88 acres) for cultivation, while the state reserved every third lot for subsequent sale with the proceeds destined for reinvestment in the colonies. [36] In 1880 and 1885 the province approved additional legislation to protect, stimulate, and organize both agricultural and stockraising activities. [37]

Under the popular assumption that Mendoza had a comparative advantage in the production of wine, olives, and walnuts, the provincial government twice passed special laws to encourage their cultivation. Stimulation of the three industries first appeared in the form of prizes with conditions attached to them that indicate a concern for quality as well as quantity. Of the 10,000 pesos set aside for awards, each cuadra of 2,000 grape plants cultivated for two years could receive 100 pesos; each 100 olive trees, 50 pesos; and each 100 walnut trees, 50 pesos. To collect on the grape prize, however, two and one-half meters had to separate each plant from north to south and from east to west, the earth clean and properly prepared, the plants alive, at least one meter high, and five centimeters thick, supported by strong wooden stakes, and in productive condition. [38] When this law failed to produce the desired results, the legislature passed a series of laws which exonerated new plantings of grapes, olives, and walnuts from all taxation. [39]

Such measures reflected the governing elites' concern with fomenting modern techniques to underwrite the province's development. In general, the public policy measures adopted between 1862 and 1885 provided for the integrated expansion of the local economy at all levels and in all traditional products as it responded to national development. Demographic expansion concentrated in the core departments with some inclination toward dispersal. [40] Agriculture grew on a uniform basis, along with an acceleration in wheat and grape production and renewed interest in planting new lands in outlying departments. [41] Only the absence of a rapid and economic transport link with the seaboard markets frustrated the province's growth in the late 1860s and early 1870s.

Still, as rail lines spread slowly throughout eastern Argentina Mendoza's export and import accounts with coastal areas rose rapidly. The province maintained its lucrative export business in cattle with Chile, but imports from the latter dropped precipitously. Cattle alone accounted for more than 90 percent of the value of all exports to Chile in most years. Imports over the Andes consisted mainly of items consumed in Mendoza: rice, sugar, yerba, coffee, and textiles. Textiles alone comprised nearly 60 percent of all imports for most years. But by the late 1870s a strong shift had occurred in this import pattern. In 1880 Mendoza imported no rice, sugar, yerba, or coffee by way of the Andes. Textiles fell dramatically in 1881 and never returned to their former levels. The importation of clothing and household articles increased but never reached the scale that textiles had achieved.[42]

An analysis of Mendoza's trading relationship with her sister provinces reveals what happened. While no peso values exist for either imports or exports through La Paz (on the border between Mendoza and San Luis) for the period 1878-84, the volume of trade can be estimated. By law, all traders had to carry *guías* (bills of lading) which described the amount and weight of each order imported or exported. Unfortunately, weights did not always appear, and those that did sometimes varied wildly even for one product in a particular container. In order to estimate missing weights for the years 1878, 1879, and 1880, an average of known weights per product and container was substituted where necessary.[43]

By 1878 Mendoza imported rice, sugar, yerba, tobacco, and coffee from the interior by rail to Villa Mercedes and by mule or oxcart from there to Mendoza. An extensive list of other products also increased in volume. They included iron, hardware, alcoholic beverages (except wine), kerosene, paper, drugs, tableware, and the undefined, catchall category of "general merchandise." With the exception of tobacco, none of these products continued on to Chile. The rising volume of goods represented an increase in consumption precipitated by renewed exports of locally produced items.

Despite the imprecision of available export and import data, certain patterns emerge whose significance did not escape some mendocinos. The progress achieved earlier in Mendoza's rural development enhanced its export potential. Both private and public initiatives focused on the seaboard markets which the railroad would open. In doing so, the mendocinos consciously sought to alter their close economic association with Chile in favor of integrating the province with the emerging coastal-national economy.[44] From a local point of view the vehicle for integration was the railroad, but the extension of rail lines throughout central Argentina also facilitated agricultural development on the pampa, a reality which threatened Mendoza's flour, corn, barley, and alfalfa. These events indicated that wine would form the backbone of Mendoza's export economy.

There began in Mendoza what one writer labeled a veritable "furor" to plant grapes in pursuit of the maxim: "To govern in Mendoza is to plant vines."[45] In the departments of Las Heras, Guaymallén, Godoy Cruz, Maipú, Luján, San Martín, and Junín the government had issued 333 licenses in 1884 to establish bodegas.[46] By 1885 the declared amount of land with vineyards had risen to 8,700 hectares, 54 percent of which lay in the departments of Guaymallén, Maipú, and Las Heras.

Many growers entered the industry in search of quick and high profits. The investment in four acres of vineyard could reach between 620 and 1,000 pesos during the four years between planting the vines and harvesting the first grapes. But from the fourth to the seventh years, by which time the vines were fully matured, net earnings on capital invested rose from 10-16 percent to 40-64 percent.[47] The initial investment seemed high, but the government relieved part of the burden by creating a tax shelter in 1881 when it absolved vineyards of all taxes for the first five years after planting.

The rush to plant grapes, however, reinforced old habits and careless methods. Despite the diffusion of modern techniques many growers continued to plant vines together with other crops, especially alfalfa. Association with the latter damaged vines by depriving them of proper nutrition and sufficient water.[48] Within the vineyards themselves growers often mixed different classes and qualities of grapes and enclosed their livestock within the vineyards after the harvest.[49] These practices led to abnormally poor crops and to very low quality wines.

Regressive actions of this nature continued to plague the province's viticultural sector for many years to come. Other difficulties that Mendoza would experience as it became integrated into the agro-export economy of the coast had already begun to appear. Nevertheless, by 1885 most mendocinos foresaw only unprecedented growth for their province once the railroad conquered the geographic isolation that had inhibited Mendoza's development in the past. Hard work, initiative, education, and supportive public policies had served the province's interests well and there seemed little reason to doubt that they would continue to do so in the future.

> And the voice of Mendoza has . . . a significance that no one will fail to recognize. It is the expression of its triumphant willingness to work, and the demand for aid so that it may continue to march; it is the offer of the riches that spring forth from its soil and the pursuit of trade with the other provinces of the republic; it is the desire to teach and to learn. . . and the outpouring of a high and noble spirit that aspires to strengthen, if it is possible, the fraternal bonds that unite the Argentine provinces.[50]

In the early 1880s many officials, both national and local, made similarly eloquent appraisals of Mendoza and its future. Beyond the obvious reasons for their high expectations lay the less discernible but everpresent traditional image of Mendoza as a manmade oasis. Since its founding the province had progressed only in relation to the inhabitants' labors. The rich soil supported many kinds of crops but only if people provided the land with water. Poplar trees lined the streets, enclosed and subdivided cultivated lands because the inhabitants planted them. Juan Cobo introduced the poplar to Mendoza in 1809, and in reward for his efforts, received a lifetime exoneration from all ordinary and extraordinary taxes. His efforts were seconded by men like Tomás Godoy Cruz, who brought silk raising to the province and Michel Pouget, who introduced, cultivated, and experimented with dozens of varieties of French grapes. [51]

Throughout the pre-railroad period mendocinos built canals, roads, and bridges; they planted fruit trees, cereals, and vegetables and raised livestock and fowl both for their own consumption and for export. Alfalfa fields were planted and irrigated to enrich the transandine cattle trade. [52] Through continuous efforts the mendocinos had created a prosperous economy based on trade and agro-exports. Only a few products such as sugar, yerba, and rice were imported along with manufactured goods. As a result, there developed in Mendoza a local pride and faith in the productive capacities of man, which Carlos Villanueva's analysis of agriculture and stockraising in Argentina reflects.

"Without doubt, the littoral lacks the necessary preparation to all of a sudden run its agricultural and stockraising industries according to the most advanced methods. . . .To work the land today, and to expect from its fertility results proportionate to our wants, it was necessary to sow seeds in its breast and to implant the required knowledge in the minds of the community yesterday. To harvest something tomorrow it is indispensable for us to set ourselves to the task. . .today, and to move the spirit of the countryside, after having shaken the cities: in the latter there is capital, and in the former, the arms to prepare the earth." [53]

Between 1861 and 1885 the mendocinos labored to rebuild their capital, to revive commerce, to modernize their economy, and to integrate their province with the coastal economy. A highly cohesive elite led these efforts on both the public and private levels. But the province also counted on an emerging middle class which supported reforms in both agriculture and industry. Generally, the elite's activities tended toward autonomous investment as they improved education, transportation, and irrigation in the province, and as they tried to modernize the wine industry. Their efforts contributed to the fairly balanced demographic and agricultural growth of the province throughout this period.

During this process some of the drawbacks of Mendoza's export economy had begun to manifest themselves. Agricultural development on the pampa diminished the prospects for exporting most of the province's traditional products. Increasingly, wine became the area's major hope, especially as unprecedented numbers of Italians and Spaniards began settling on the coast. But the careless methods used by all too many wine producers weakened the prospects for success. The railroad appeared as the "savior" as it tied the province into seaboard markets. Fluctuations in the national economy had sent economic shockwaves through Mendoza in the past, however, and the close linkage of the provincial and littoral economies would magnify the effect of future cycles. Nevertheless, the inauguration of a railroad to the province in 1885 seemed to represent limitless possibilities for development. Reaching for those possibilities, however, would prove to be far more complicated and complex than anyone imagined at the beginning of Mendoza's first modern boom.

Endnotes for Chapter 2

1. Several authors have analyzed this period of oligarchic family rule, including: Pedro Santos Martínez C., "Mendoza, 1862-1892: Ensayo de interpretación sociopolítica," *Contribuciones para la historia de Mendoza,* ed. Pedro Santos Martínez C. (Mendoza, 1969), pp. 1131-74; Luis Campoy, "Persistencia de algunas valores sociales en una sociedad en desarrollo," *Investigaciones en Sociología,* 4th yr., no. 9 (January-June 1965): 53-84; and Lucio Funes, *Gobernadores de Mendoza: La Oligarquía* (Mendoza, 1942).

2. Seymour Martin Lipset and Aldo Solari, eds., *Elites in Latin America* (New York, 1967), p. viii. A similar argument is made by José Medina Echavarría, "A Theoretical Model of Development Applicable to Latin America," in Egbert de De Vries and José M. Echavarría, eds., *Social Aspects of Economic Development in Latin America,* 2 vols., UNESCO, Technology and Society Series (Tournai, Belgium, 1963), 1:35.

3. F. Ignacio Rickard, *A Mining Journal Across the Great Andes* (London, England, 1863), pp. 109-12.

4. Llerena, "Cuadros descriptivos," *Revista de Buenos Aires* 11 (1866): 71. Biographical data on the author is from Masini Calderón, *Mendoza hace cien años,* pp. 9-10. For related data see: Miguel Rogelio Tristany, *Guía estadística de la provincia de Mendoza* (Mendoza, 1860), pp. 93-4. República Argentina, Ministerio de Hacienda, *Memoria,* 1863, n.p.

5. Tristany, *Guía estadística,* pp. 62-4, and table between pp. 8-9.

6. The following discussion of the 1864 census is based on Llerena, "Cuadros descriptivos," 10:588-92, and 11:62-76.

7. Guillermo J. Cano, *Régimen jurídico económico de las aguas en Mendoza,* 1810-1884 (Mendoza, 1941), pp. 42-3; and "Mensaje," Arístides Villanueva, Governor, *ROM,* 1872, pp. 346-8.

8. For additional information on the period 1810-84, see: Cano, *Régimen jurídico;* and Agustín García, *La irrigación en la Provincia de Mendoza* (Mendoza, 1902). For the colonial period see Santos Martínez, C., "La irrigación de Mendoza durante el Virreinato (1776-1810)," *Revista de la Junta de Estudios Históricos Mendoza,* 2d ser., 1st yr., no. 1 (1961): 46-68.

9. Provincial Decrees of 21 January 1864; 23 September 1864; and 15 December 1864.

10. Provincial Decree of 28 April 1854, and Provincial Law of 29 December 1870.

11. National Decree of 14 June 1872, and Provincial Decree of 12 October 1872.

12. Provincial Decree of 23 January 1875.

13. Provincia de Mendoza, *Memoria para el año* 1879 (Mendoza, 1880), p. 158.

14. Provincial Law of 27 April 1882; and Provincia de Mendoza, *La Provincia de Mendoza en su Exposición Interprovincial de 1885* (Mendoza, 1885), pp. 97-9. The census was taken on 31 December 1882.

15. José M. Segura, *Mensaje del Gobernador de la Provincia a la H. Cámara Lejislativa al declarar abierto el primer período ordinario de sesiones de 1883* (Mendoza, 1883), p. 13. Hereafter these published versions of the semiannual addresses will be cited as: governor, *Mensaje,* (period of session, year), pages(s).

16. Provincial Law of 16 December 1884.

17. For examples of the importance which the government assigned to both education and irrigation see: Arístedes Villanueva, "Mensaje," *ROM,* 1872, pp. 346-8; and Francisco Civit, "Mensaje," *ROM,* 1876, pp. 458-70.

18. Provincial Law of 11 June 1872.

19. Provincial Decree of 21 February 1872, and Accord of the same date.

20. National Law of 8 September 1870; Provincial Decree of 13 May 1872; and Provincial Law of 11 June 1872.

21. F. Civit, "Mensaje," *ROM,* 1876, p. 288.

22. "Circular" dated 18 April 1876, reprinted in *ROM,* 1876, pp. 381-3.

23. Provincial Law of 15 May 1876, and Provincial Decree of 17 May 1876.

24. Provincial Decrees of 2 January 1873, and 15 May 1876.

25. For example: Aaron Pavlowsky, *Conferencia sobre vitivinicultura* (San Juan, 1885); *Informe sobre los trabajos ejecutados en la Escuela Nacional de Agricultural de Mendoza en el año de 1884* (Mendoza, 1885); and *La viticultura en la República Argentina* (Mendoza, 1888).

26. Mendoza, *Exposición Interprovincial,* p. 76.

27. The *ROM* is replete with laws and decrees referring to transport improvements between 1864 and 1884. For examples of internal improvements as they relate first to the Central Argentino and later to the Gran Oeste Argentino see: A Villanueva, "Mensaje," *ROM,* 1871, p. 283; and J. Segura, *Mensaje* (I, 1883), pp. 19-24.

28. Characterizations of the province's main products and its general agricultural richness in themselves demonstrate balanced growth throughout the period 1864-85 by their remarkable consistency. See for example: Tristany, *Guía estadística,* pp. 60-1; Martin de Moussy, *Description geographique,* 2:478; and 3:456-7; Llerena, "Cuadros descriptivos," 10:589; de Elia, *Memoria,* p. 42; Republica Argentina, Departamento Nacional de Agricultura, *Informe,* 1872 (Buenos Aires, 1873), pp. 16-17; and Pavlowsky, *Informe,* pp. 4, 13.

29. Provincial Decree of 12 November 1867.

30. Provincial Decree of 26 February 1872.

31. For a summary of these projects see: "Los agrimensores y la propiedad raíz," *Los Andes,* 26 April 1900, p. 4.

32. Provincial Law of 6 December 1870. Mendocinos won prizes at the Córdoba exposition for their exhibits of dried fruits, marble, cotton, wine, coal, oil, minerals, hams, brandy, and porcelain. Mulhall, *Handbook* (1885), p. 198.

33. Comisión Directora de la Exposición Nacional en Córdoba, *Boletín,* 4 vols. (Buenos Aires, 1869-72), 2:462.

34. Provincial Decree of 15 November 1873.

35. Provincial Decree of 7 September 1874. In the same year Franklin and Ciriaco Guevara received the right to work 60 square leagues of state land in San Rafael for three years. They paid 1,670 pesos for the permit. Contract of 10 October 1874.

36. Provincial Law of 12 April 1875.

37. Provincial Law of 12 May 1880, for example, treated longstanding problems such as pasturage rights, fencing, legal culpability, water rights, brands, mule and oxcart traffic through unfenced areas, and the like.

38. Provincial Law of 7 September 1874, and Provincial Degree of 15 September 1874.

39. Provincial Laws of 23 August 1881, and 18 September 1881.

40. Mendoza, *Exposición Interprovincial,* p. 14; *Primer Censo Nacional* (1869), pp. 346-7; *Segundo Censo Nacional* (1895), 2:369; *Registro Estadístico de la República Argentina* (1864), p. 19; Llerena, "Cuadros descriptivos," 10:591; Martin de Moussy, *Description geographique,* 3:459-60; and Paz Soldán, *Diccionario geográfico,* p. 66.

41. Llerena, "Cuadros descriptivos," 10:589-90; *Registro estadístico* (1872-3), pp. 606-7; and Mendoza, *Anuario,* 1884, p. 49.

42. República Argentina, *Estadística General de Comercio Exterior,* 1874, pp. 423-4; 1884, pp. XII, XIV; 1895, pp. 257, 260; and *Registro Estadístico,* 1868, p. 320.

43. Mendoza, *Anuario, 1884,* p. 49; Mendoza, *Estadística general,* 1882, p. 23; and Argentina, *Estadística de la República Argentina,* 1872-3, pp. 606-7.

44. According to Kermann Burmeister, a German who lived in Mendoza for a year (1857-58), an effort to shift the trade pattern had begun by 1857. He noted that several local firms had been established in Rosario to handle commerce with Europe which used to cross the Andes. He claimed that several "Chilean" exports to Europe were actually from Mendoza. The branches in Rosario may have reinforced the decision of the Central Argentino's promoters to build a station at the key postroad junction of Villa Nueva. Burmeister, *Viaje por los Estados de Plata* (Buenos Aires, 1943), p. 218. The original work appeared in German in 1861.

45. C. Villanueva, *El litoral y el interior,* p. 129fn., and Juan Aguirre's preface to E. Civit, *Los viñedos,* p. 5. The slogan alludes to Juan B. Alberdi's popular dictum "To govern is to populate" made in reference to Argentina's need for immigrants.

46. Mendoza, *Anuario,* n.p.

47. Pavlowsky, *Informe,* p. 14.

48. Pavlowsky, *Conferencia sobre viticultura,* pp. 19-20.

49. Blanco, "Las viñas," pp. 215, 222.

50. M. Vázquez de la Morena, "Exposición interprovincial en mendoza," *Boletín del Departamento Nacional de Agricultura,* 8 (31 October 1884): 667.

51. Blanco, "Las viñas," p. 218fn., and Tristany, *Guía estadística,* p. 6.

52. On Mendoza's economy during the latter part of the colonial period see: Pedro Santos Martínez C., *Historia económica de Mendoza durante el virreinato, 1776-1810* (Madrid, Spain, 1961).

53. C. Villanueva, *El litoral y el interior,* p. 122.

Chapter 3

Continuity and Change:

Mendoza's Economy under National Growth, 1885-1914

Development in Mendoza before 1914 favored the rapidly expanding wine industry but also stimulated the province's traditional agricultural and stockraising sectors. Throughout this period Mendoza continued to produce sufficient supplies of agricultural and livestock products for both its own needs and for export. Although the wine industry focused on the large consumer markets of Rosario and Buenos Aires, by 1914 Mendoza had widened its commercial network to include most of the central and northern provinces in the country.[1]

As the provincial economy expanded, the intensification of land use in the core departments led to the dispersal of agriculture and stockraising into the large peripheral departments. The central departments concentrated on grape cultivation, wine production, and commerce. These changes in the province's land use pattern originated in the organization of the area's transport network, the government's administration of water resources, the demographic growth of the core, and the importance of wine exports in the local economy.

The process of continuity and change in the structure of Mendoza's economy took place in two successive stages. Under the influence of the recently inaugurated railroad and the general prosperity of the national economy, the mendocinos worked to bring thousands of hectares of new land into production. Demographic expansion and an increase in specialization provided for moderate growth in commercial agriculture. The need for draft animals for internal transportation, a rise in demand for meat, and the continued prosperity of the transandine cattle trade benefited stockraising. During this first stage (1885-1902) the concentration of viticulture and winemaking in the commercial center of the province began to displace the less intensive agricultural and livestock activities.

Toward the end of the century two factors that lay beyond local control brought this initial period of expansion to a close. In 1897 a tariff imposed by Chile on cattle imports from Argentina sent Mendoza's profitable trading relationship with her transandine neighbor into a prolonged recession. Concurrently, a national financial crisis in the 1890s resulted in the reduction of consumer demand for Mendoza's wine in coastal markets. The stabilization of wine exports occurred at a time when large numbers of newly planted vineyards reached their full maturity. The subsequent drop in grape prices produced a commercial panic between 1901 and 1902 that temporarily depressed the wine industry.

However, as the national economy entered a second boom, the local railroad completed several branch lines, and the Chilean situation improved, the provincial economy quickly recovered from the wine crisis and a second period of prosperity began. During this stage (1903-14) immigration reached unprecedented levels, cattle exports to Chile revived, and corn, barley, and alfalfa production increased. Competition from pampa farms induced a sharp decline in wheat cultivation. The wine industry overshadowed all other sectors as the cultivation of grapes and the elaboration and exportation of wine advanced at rapid rates.

The progress of Mendoza's export economy after 1903 reinforced the trend in changing land use patterns that had emerged during the first stage. When the Gran Oeste completed a branch line to San Rafael, this fertile southern department with its virtually untapped water resources experienced rapid growth. Eventually, San Rafael would become a second major pole in the geographic distribution of rural production, especially after the Pacífico and Oeste railroads also built branches into the area. But another national recession, caused in part by the international events that preceded World War I, contributed to a second slump in Mendoza's economy after 1912.

For the purposes of analysis, the province's sixteen departments are divided into five groups: the Capital, Guaymallén, and Godoy Cruz (Group I); Maipú, and Luján (Group II); San Martín, Junín, and Rivadavia (Group III); Las Heras, Lavalle, Santa Rosa, La Paz, San Carlos, Tunuyán, and Tupungato (Group IV); and San Rafael, which included the contemporary departments of Malargüe and General Alvear (Group V). The eight departments represented by Groups I, II, and III held roughly 3 percent of the province's total surface area (15,365,000 hectares); the seven departments in Group IV contained 37 percent; and San Rafael covered 60 percent of the province.[2]

Between 1885 and 1903 cultivation of three of Mendoza's main crops (wheat, corn, barley, and alfalfa) increased moderately. Wheat suffered occasional fluctuations as the province lost some markets for its flour exports to the rapidly expanding farms on the pampa. Barley changed little while corn and alfalfa expanded steadily. By the turn of the century, wheat, corn, and alfalfa sowings had risen at average annual rates of 2.7 percent, 15.8 percent, and 3.7 percent, respectively.[3]

The expansion of alfalfa production supported both a profitable trade in alfalfa seed for exportation and the growth of Mendoza's livestock sectors. Between 1888 and 1903 the number of livestock in Mendoza increased 37 percent. Cattle comprised the majority of these herds, although its share dropped from 43 percent to 33 percent. The decline originated in a recession in the transandine trade and in the rapid increase of horsebreeding and mulebreeding. In response to the transport needs of the population and of the wine industry, the number of horses and mules raised locally more than doubled during the first stage.[4]

As anticipated by the pre-1880s governing elite in Mendoza, the production and exportation of wine became the province's main industry. Aided by the arrival of nearly 1,200,000 immigrants, mostly Italians and Spaniards, Argentina's population increased by over 2,000,000 inhabitants between 1885 and 1903.[5] Most of the newcomers settled on the coast, especially in and around the federal capital, but developers also established agricultural colonies on the pampa in Santa Fe Province. With the impetus provided by rail links to these consumer markets the mendocinos set out more than 19,000 hectares of vines.[6] Wine exports soared from 24,000 hectoliters (hls.) to cover 1,000,000 hls. by 1902 (1 hectoliter equals slightly less than 25 gallons).[7]

During the initial years of Mendoza's development the geographic distribution of rural production represented a continuation of the pattern discussed in Chapter 2. Water from the Mendoza and Tunuyán Rivers provided for the irrigation of land devoted to agriculture and viticulture. Farmers preferred to locate near the commercial routes to the other provinces and to Chile. Livestock roamed the large southwestern and southern departments where ranchers fattened cattle for shipment over the Andes. These three factors--transportation, irrigation, and trade--exercised a strong influence on Mendoza's land use patterns during the latter part of the century.

The productive potential of Mendoza's rural economy had influenced the decision of entrepreneurs and the national government to build a railroad to the province.[8] Both they and national authorities projected a route that paralleled the oxcart trails from San Luis in the east and San Juan in the north. For part of its length the railroad also followed the Tunuyán River and then crossed through the area most extensively irrigated by the Mendoza River. As a result, those activities closely related to trade tended to locate near the means of transportation and irrigation, in this case, in the core departments.

However, because of the overexploitation of the Mendoza River by agriculturalists, the provincial authorities placed severe restrictions on its use for irrigation. In the Ley de Aguas (Water Law) of 1884 the government specifically forbade any new taps of the river.[9] The Canal Zanjón, which fed water from the Mendoza River into the area east of the Capital, came under similar restrictions. Through the use of official inspectors the government controlled access to the Tunuyán River in the core departments but did not prevent its use for irrigation.

These general factors, the trajectory of the railroad and the government's administration of water resources, led to a shift in the distribution of rural production. The rapid expansion of the wine industry and the demographic growth of the departments in Group I reinforced the trend. The areas outside the core began to develop their agricultural and viticultural sectors. With the exception of mule breeding, livestock activities moved almost totally into the large outlying departments. The demand for mules to transport grapes to bodegas and wine to the railroad provided for an increase in this sector in the core departments.

In 1888 both commercial agriculture and viticulture concentrated in the zones around the Capital. The eight central departments that comprise Groups I, II, and III accounted for two-thirds of the wheat and alfalfa planted and more than three-fourths of the corn and barley. Nearly all of the grape fields appeared in the central departments. Still basically a frontier area, the southern department of San Rafael contained 1 percent of the corn, alfalfa, and vineyards; 3 percent of the barley; and 11 percent of the wheat cultivated in the province. Stockraising exhibited the reverse situation with the traditional grazing departments of Groups IV and V dominating the sector. Led by Tunuyán, Tupungato, San Carlos, and San Rafael, the two groups reported 77 percent of the cattle, 68 percent of the sheep, and 87 percent of the goats raised in the province.

By 1903 agriculture had shifted away from the Capital in three directions. The department of Lavalle increased its area planted with wheat and corn from 700 hectares in 1895 to 2,700 hectares in 1903. Most of the increase came along the northern border with Maipú, where producers could benefit from the Mendoza River, partially liberated from the ban of 1884. A second shift occurred toward the southeast along the Tunuyán River and the Gran Oeste's rails. There, the departments in Group III increased their alfalfa and corn sowings in support of an export trade. During the first six months of 1903, the province exported nearly 6,000 tons of alfalfa seed, and 1,500 tons of corn.[10] In the southwest, and also along the Tunuyán River, a third shift benefited San Carlos, Tunuyán and Tupungato. In these three departments corn and wheat plantings between 1895 and 1903 had increased from 1,800 hectares to 5,100 hectares.

The development of alfalfa production in the regions south of the core departments and in San Rafael accompanied the continuous growth of stockraising. Between 1888 and 1903 the four departments of Tunuyán, Tupungato, San Carlos, and San Rafael added more than 45,000 hectares to alfalfa cultivation. By the turn of the century Groups IV and V contained between 80 percent and 90 percent of the cattle, sheep, goats, and horses raised in Mendoza.

In general, livestock production expanded with the first wave of prosperity that accompanied the inauguration of the railroad but receded after 1897 when the Chilean government passed an import tax on Argentine cattle.[11] While the tariff was designed primarily to protect Chile's own burgeoning livestock sectors, it also reflected a revival of agitation between the two countries over their common border. The problem was resolved in 1902, but by 1901 both sides had begun to prepare for war.[12] In that year the cattle tariff rose to between 12 and 16 gold pesos per head for steers and oxen.[13] The value of steers in Mendoza fluctuated widely according to the quality and age of the animal, but for the very best animals the tax represented about one-third of their value.[14]

The tariff had an immediate and disastrous effect on Mendoza's commercial relationship with Chile because of the singular importance of livestock in transandine trading. In most years cattle, sheep, horses, and mules exported to Chile had accounted for 99 percent of the value of all of Mendoza's transandine exports. Cattle, the most numerous and valuable of livestock shipments, numbered between 50,000 and 70,000 head annually until 1896 and then dropped sharply to 1,000 head in 1899.[15]

The near elimination of traditional nonlivestock exports to Chile and the minimal level of imports over the Andes in prior years reflected the integration of Mendoza into the national economy. The trend in exports began in the early 1880s and was reinforced by the agricultural and mineral development in Chile. During the last two decades of the nineteenth century Mendoza shipped ostrich feathers, wool, hides, soap, silver, and copper ore to Chile only in odd years. Although the records do not indicate the composition of imports, the total value of imports shows that Mendoza had a very favorable trade balance with her transandine neighbor. Between 1885 and 1890 imports rose from 11,000 gold pesos to 66,000 gold pesos. But this increase probably resulted from the purchase of equipment by the Gran Oeste Railroad in the late 1880s. Subsequently, imports declined to 3,000 gold pesos in 1896 and 1897 and remained at less than 10,000 gold pesos for most years through 1908.

Within Argentina wine quickly rose to a dominant position among Mendoza's exports. During the first stage of the industry's development exporters shipped wine to just seven markets. In 1894, for example, the federal capital and Rosario received 41 percent and 21 percent, respectively, of the 261,000 hls. shipped from Mendoza. The rural areas outside of these two cities consumed 6 percent and 8 percent of the wine shipments while the provinces of Córdoba, San Luis, Santiago del Estero, and Tucumán accounted for the remainder.[16]

The wine industry's success overshadowed all other products, but many of Mendoza's traditional exports also prospered. Compared with the annual reports for 1883, the records for the first six months of 1902 demonstrate that of sixteen major items, only flour had declined in volume during the intervening years. Alcohol, wheat, and corn advanced from less than 30 tons each in 1883 to more than 1,200 tons for the six months reported for 1902. Alfalfa seed rose from 96 to 5,600 tons; hides, from 189 to 652 tons; and grapes reached the unusual level of over 13,000 tons.[17]

The volume of grape exports in 1902 indicated that the industry had entered a severe crisis. Both grape and wine prices declined while sources of credit tightened after the turn of the century causing a panic in the commercial and export sectors. Grape prices fell from an average of 7.07$m/n (paper pesos) per 100 kilos (218 lbs.) in 1900 to 2.39$m/n per 100 kilos in 1901 and 2.72$m/n in 1902.[18] Wine in Buenos Aires sometimes sold for less than at the bodega in Mendoza and San Juan.[19] Part of the problem lay in the insecurity of littoral markets, where a drop in cattle exports, financial depression, and a scarcity of foreign capital restrained commercial activities.[20]

In 1903 the national government, at the request of Mendoza, sent a commission to investigate the causes of the crisis. The chairman of the commission, Pedro Arata, claimed that rising property values, easy credit, and high profits had generated a wave of speculation in the wine industry during the 1880s and 1890s that finally broke in 1900.[21] The commission also found that investors often lacked the requisite technical ability or the interest for making wine. As a result, many bodegas began to produce and to sell wines of the lowest quality, which did nothing to assuage a skeptical consuming public.

The shortcomings in the export and sale of wine magnified the deficiencies of production. Many exporters failed to take into account the specific demands of their markets, and anarchy reigned in the commercialization of the product itself. Producers would send wine to Buenos Aires unsold, thus losing all control over its prices. They had no fixed clientele, selling to storeowners, wine blenders, wholesalers, and retailers as chance determined. The growers contributed to the crisis by consistently mixing distinct varieties of grapes in one vineyard and by failing to exercise any standards of quality control over their products. [22]

The commission's analysis came as no surprise to progressive elements in the province who had issued similar warnings periodically during the first stage of Mendoza's development. [23] By 1902, however, the prosperity of the provincial economy depended heavily on the state of the wine industry. Its recession sent shockwaves through the entire economy, leading to a general paralysis of commerce and industry. [24] For example, in 1903 there were 124 fewer business establishments in the province than in 1902, and the number of bodegas in the same two years dropped by one-half. [25]

Arata's commission made a series of recommendations designed to reactivate the industry. In accordance with their proposals, the national government abolished its tax on wine, and the provincial government eased its tax on vineyards. [26] Concurrently, some producers began to improve the quality of their wine. Oenologists analyzed the composition of both foreign and national wines to identify the shortcomings of the local products. [27]

While the commission had succinctly presented several longstanding problems in both grape cultivation and wine production, it had only indirectly touched on the real origin of the crisis. In the early 1890s viticulturalists had set out several thousand hectares of vines. These vineyards came to full maturity around the turn of the century when wine exports stabilized. Only grape production really suffered from the recession because of a reduced demand by winemakers for grapes during these record harvests.

Because of the national financial crisis of the 1890s the Gran Oeste Railroad had delayed its plans to expand within Mendoza. But in 1902 the company began a construction program that opened up the fertile southern department of San Rafael to development and benefited the commercial agriculture and viticulture sectors in the core departments. Between 1885 and 1901 the railroad laid a total of 100 kilometers in its system. During the next nine years the line added 327 kilometers of rails. Most of the increase was registered by the completion of a 185 kilometer branch line to San Rafael while the rest of the new track appeared in the core departments and around the Capital. In addition, a merger between the Gran Oeste and Pacífico railroads in 1907 brought an immediate increase in capital and rolling stock to the line that greatly improved the Gran Oeste's ability to provide efficient and economical service to Mendoza's producers. [28]

The expansionist policies of all the railroad companies added more than 8,000 kilometers of track to the national network between 1900 and 1909 and fostered commerce throughout the country. [29] Most of this increase occurred on the fertile pampa where wheat and beef production led Argentina into a second period of rapid growth. Attracted by the opportunities that the agricultural exploitation of the pampa seemed to offer, immigrants began arriving in far greater numbers than at any time since the late 1880s. Net annual immigration to Argentina rose from 38,000 in 1904 to 94,000 in 1905 and ranged from 120,000 to nearly 200,000 during the next five years.[30] Some of these immigrants, mainly Spaniards and Italians, settled in Mendoza. The newcomers provided the province with skilled and semiskilled laborers to work the new vineyards and bodegas.

But as a result of the generally favorable atmosphere for personal advancement that Mendoza offered, many of their numbers also invested in commerce, viticulture, and agriculture. Between 1890 and 1905 seldom did more than 2,000 immigrants enter the province in any single year. Then over the next eight years the annual rate frequently surpassed 10,000 and reached highs of 15,000 and 16,000 before descending sharply in 1914 and 1915.[31]

The volume of immigrants and the settlement pattern they followed had a significant effect on the demographic growth of Mendoza. The number of inhabitants in the province between 1895 and 1914 had increased by 41 percent. Most of this rise occurred during the period of high immigration and resulted in the creation of two main demographic poles in the province. The immigrants who settled in the Capital between 1907 and 1913 accounted for 71 percent of the city's 1914 population.[32] In San Rafael the construction of branch lines by the Pacífico and Oeste railroads in 1911 and 1912, respectively, had fostered an acceleration in the department's rate of growth. By 1914 newly arrived immigrants represented 40 percent of the department's population, most of which centered around the city of San Rafael, where farmers and ranchers used the Diamante and Atuel Rivers for irrigation. This area alone held almost as many people as the eight departments in Group IV.

Where Mendoza's immigrants chose to reside reflects both their interests and the changing structure of the provincial economy. Foreigners in Mendoza, especially Spaniards and Italians, invested primarily in commerce and the wine industry. In 1893 Argentines owned 72 percent of the 429 bodegas in the province, but by 1914 they accounted for just 31 percent of 1,507 bodegas.[33] In a less spectacular way, the immigrants also took control of grape production. Argentines owned 71 percent of the 1,770 vineyards in Mendoza in 1895 but only 48 percent of the 6,160 vineyards recorded in 1914.[34]

By both number of establishments and capital invested foreigners likewise dominated commerce. Of a total of 1,169 businesses in the province in 1909, Argentines owned 27 percent while Spaniards, Italians, and Arabs, together accounted for 65 percent. This distribution changes very little according to capital invested. Native Argentines held 22 percent and Spaniards, Italians, and Arabs, 66 percent of the 18,500,000$m/n which the commercial establishments represented.[35]

The erosion of local control over various sectors of Mendoza's economy extended somewhat into agriculture, but not at all into stockraising. Argentines accounted for 86 percent and Italians, Spaniards, and Frenchmen, 1 percent each of a total of 3,081 rural proprietors in Mendoza in 1888.[36] In 1914 Argentines still monopolized stockraising with 76 percent of all ranches (2,167). The foreign-born, however, had entered agriculture. By 1914 they owned a majority of cereal farms with 53 percent of the 704 farms recorded in that year. But partly as a result of their livestock interests, Argentines held a majority of the alfalfa fields with 59 percent of 805 establishments. [37]

Immigration, transportation improvements, and a booming national economy formed the base for another thrust in Mendoza's development. During this second stage (1904-14) the pattern of continuity and change in the province's economy that had emerged during the first stage continued with relatively little variation. The same elements of transportation, irrigation, and trade that had played a major role in the distribution of production before 1900 reinforced the trend during the second stage. Commerce, grape cultivation, and wine production intensified in the core departments while agriculture moved into the peripheral departments. The only exception to this pattern occurred in the southern region of San Rafael. Agriculturalists and viticulturalists in search of new land and a more ample water supply than the central departments offered followed the Gran Oeste into San Rafael. By 1914 this department had become the most important agricultural and livestock department in the province and occupied a major place in the wine industry.

The growth of Mendoza's population, commercial sectors, and wine industry led to an increase in internal demand for agricultural and livestock products. Between 1907 and 1914 the area cultivated with corn had risen 20 percent; with barley, 89 percent; and with alfalfa, 38 percent. Only wheat failed to prosper as it suffered a precipitous decline between 1907 and 1908 of 76 percent, but then it stabilized for the remainder of the second stage. [38] By this time, the development of wheat farming on the pampa had not only eliminated most of Mendoza's traditional flour markets but had also begun to invade consumer centers within the province.

Internal demand and a release from the depressive effects of the Chilean tariff after the Treaty of 1902 fomented the rapid development of stockraising. Between 1903 and 1914 ranchers added nearly 400,000 head to their herds. San Rafael initiated a prosperous wool export industry and by 1914 held 83 percent of the sheep raised in Mendoza. [39] Four years earlier the department had shipped 91 percent of the 620 tons of wool exported from the province. Meanwhile, the transandine cattle trade recovered from the disastrous recession of the final years of conflict between Chile and Argentina. By 1912 the value of cattle shipments over the Andes reached an all-time high of 1,850,000 gold pesos.

The conclusive displacement of the core departments by the large outlying departments in agricultural production took place during the second stage. While viticulturalists and wine producers continued to locate in the province's commercial center, the demographic growth of the core placed additional demands on the area's water resources. Thus, the less intensive agricultural sectors extended their activities along the lower reaches of the Tunuyán River in the departments of San Carlos, Tunuyán, and Tupungato. As noted earlier, the development of San Rafael contributed significantly to this trend.

The only exception to the tendency of agriculture to disperse away from the central departments occurred with the rise of alfalfa cultivation in Group III. San Martín, Junín, and Rivadavia, together added 18,000 hectares to their alfalfa farms between 1907 and 1911. Thus, unchanged from its 1903 position, Group III accounted for one-fourth of the provincial total. As in the first stage, the prosperity of alfalfa production in these departments originated in the provision of seed for exportation and of feed for the draft animals used in the wine industry.

After a near cessation of new plantings between 1901 and 1902, the expansion of Mendoza's vineyards resumed its precrisis rate until 1907. Then, with massive immigration, a relaxation of credit, and improved transport facilities, investors exhibited an unabashed drive to plant new vineyards. By 1914 grapevines extended over 70,000 hectares, an increase of 170 percent over the 1903 figure. While the eight core departments intensified their specialization in grape growing, their relative position declined. The three groups added 31,000 hectares to their 1903 total (19,000) but dropped from 83 to 72 percent of the industry. San Rafael had expanded its vineyards by over 10,000 hectares and its share of the provincial sum from 9 to 18 percent. Group IV moved up to 10 percent of the industry as Las Heras doubled its vineyards to 2,000 hectares, and San Carlos advanced from 93 hectares to 1,800 hectares.[40]

Despite the predominance of wine in commerce, Mendoza continued to ship agricultural goods, hides, and wool to the other provinces. Of sixteen items listed in the accounts for 1902 and 1903, only five consistently appear in the records for the period 1905-10: wine, alcohol, alfalfa seed, hides, and wool. But the absence of the other products may stem more from the skewed concern of local officials with the wine industry than it does from a depression in their trade.[41]

According to the provincial revenue reports from the five years, wheat and flour exports ceased while alfalfa seed shipments declined sharply. Given the reduction in acreage planted with wheat after 1907, both wheat and flour exports undoubtedly stopped during the second stage. Alfalfa seed shipments dropped from 5,750 tons in the first six months of 1903 to just 300 tons for the twelve months of 1905. The fall is so abrupt as to put the fiscal records in doubt as a true reflection of the status of the industry, although competition from alfalfa farms on the pampa could explain the depression.[42]

Both the hide and wool trades prospered after the turn of the century while a variety of other items, which appear in the 1910 reports, confirm the diversity of Mendoza's export economy. Hide shipments fluctuated around 1,000 tons annually and wool, around 500 tons annually between 1905 and 1910. In the latter year the province also exported wheat, beeswax, horsehair, dried fruit, and barley. Alfalfa seed shipments rose to 625 tons; and wool, to 650 tons in 1911.

Wine exports advanced evenly until 1907, when they began an impressive climb. From 1905 to 1907 wine shipments rose from 136,000 to 153,000 tons, and then soared to 350,000 tons by 1913. Grape exports initially dropped after their unusual highs of 1902 and 1903 when producers shipped directly to consumer markets to avoid the depressed prices offered by wine makers. Then, between 1910 and 1911, grape shipments rose from 2,700 tons to 4,850 tons and stayed at about 4,250 tons over the next three years.[43]

As the consumer markets on the coast expanded, largely as a result of massive immigration, the federal capital and Buenos Aires Province increased their share of Mendoza's wine exports. The only data available on a market basis during this period is from the first six months of 1911. But wine exports varied little on a semiannual basis in normal years.[44] The report showed that the federal capital received 41 percent, and Buenos Aires Province, 25 percent of the 64,750 tons of wine shipped from Mendoza. Compared with 1894, their combined percentage had risen from 47 percent to 64 percent. Accordingly, every other province reported in 1894 diminished in relative importance by 1911.

These figures, however, mask both the expansion of Mendoza's industry into new markets and the increased volume of wine consumed by traditional markets. In 1894 the province exported to the federal capital and to the provinces of Buenos Aires, Santa Fe, Córdoba, Tucumán, San Luis, and Santiago del Estero. After the turn of the century Mendoza added to the above markets the provinces of Catamarca, Jujuy, La Rioja, Salta, Chaco, Rio Negro, and La Pampa.[45]

The core departments had become the hub of the commercialization of Mendoza's exportable products. According to the distribution of exports by department in 1910, Groups I, II, and III, accounted for two-thirds to all of the alfalfa, honey, dried fruit, walnuts, barley, grapes, and wine shipped from the province. Only San Rafael's importance as a stockraising center offered an exception to this pattern. Among the departments, the Capital and San Martín occupied the most important positions as export centers.[46]

Before the railroad's inauguration Mendoza's population, commercial activities, industries, farms, and vineyards were situated in the eight core departments. Stockraising was located in the southwestern and southern departments. Within the core the Capital monopolized commerce, and together with Godoy Cruz and Guaymallén accounted for most of the population. The latter two departments plus Maipú and Luján held most of the vineyards. San Martín, Junín, and Rivadavia specialized in agriculture, grape cultivation, and to some extent, stockraising. The system operated in accordance with the composition of Mendoza's trading relationship with both Chile and the provinces. Rural production in the core supplied a wide range of goods for export and local consumption while the southwestern and southern departments provided livestock for Chile.

By 1914 the eight core departments still held most of the population, commercial activities, and vineyards but had lost their agricultural importance to the periphery. In addition, the opening of the south through the extension of a branch rail line to San Rafael created a second economic pole within the provincial economy. San Rafael produced a major share of the livestock, crops, and grapes; had a larger population than other departments outside of the Capital; and contributed significantly to Mendoza's exports.

As before, the structure functioned on the basis of exports but with the difference that wine by itself determined the prosperity of trade relations, and hence, of the other sectors of the internal economy. The demographic, commercial, and industrial growth of the core responded largely to the rapidly developing wine industry. What remained of stockraising and agriculture in the core supplied local consumer markets and filled the transport requirements of the wine industry within the province.

Mendoza's export pattern altered radically between 1885 and 1914. The transandine cattle trade suffered boom and bust cycles according to the state of diplomatic relations between Argentina and Chile as well as the success of Chile's protectionist policies. Nonlivestock shipments over the Andes ceased completely as local producers turned toward internal markets or abandoned traditional activities. Mendoza continued to export significant amounts of agricultural and livestock products to national markets, but wine exports quickly surpassed the other goods in importance.

Toward the end of the nineteenth century Mendoza sent wine to only a few provinces outside of the littoral. Throughout the second stage of Mendoza's development the province widened its markets to include most of the central, northern, and eastern sections of the country. Nevertheless, due to their large populations, the Capital and Buenos Aires Province consumed most of Mendoza's wine exports.

By 1914 Mendoza had become an integral part of the national economy, largely through the development of the province's wine industry. Between 1888 and 1914 Mendoza expanded its share of the total national area set out with vines from 26 percent to 60 percent. The tremendous growth of crop farming and stockraising on the humid pampa dwarfed the development of Mendoza's rural areas and the province lost ground to the national totals for most products. Its percentage of the total area cultivated in the country dropped by one-third between 1888 and 1914. Wheat farming declined during the first part of the twentieth century, but corn cultivation remained unchanged. In livestock production the province increased its portion of the national totals for all sectors including cattle. The most significant advances occurred in goat and mule breeding for which the province had widened its role from 2.7 percent for each sector in 1888 to 4.5 percent and 5.5 percent, respectively, in 1914. [47]

Transportation, irrigation, and trade formed the general forces behind the elements of continuity and change in Mendoza's economy. However, these factors only represented structural opportunities for growth. The railroad provided access to consumer markets; demand offered possibilities for trade; and water resources permitted the cultivation and production of goods to export. The success of Mendoza's economic development after 1885 depended on the decisions and actions of local entrepreneurs and the provincial government. Economic decisionmaking in these areas shaped Mendoza's response to the opportunities presented by the rapidly expanding agro-export economy of the nation and to the pressures brought to bear on the local economy by national and international forces.

Endnotes for Chapter 3

1. For two popular contrary views to this theme see: Aldo Ferrer, *La economía argentina* (Buenos Aires, 1974), pp. 123-50; and Roque M. Ferraro, *El desarrollo regional argentino* (Buenos Aires, 1973), p. 19.

2. Calculated from: Mendoza, *Memoria de la Oficina de Estadística de 1903* (Mendoza, 1903), p. 111.

3. This discussion of agricultural development in Mendoza is based on an analysis of data appearing in: Francisco Latzina, *Geografía de la República Argentina* (Buenos Aires, 1888), pp. 389-90; Latzina, *L'agriculture et l'elevage dans le Republique Argentine* (Buenos Aires, 1889), pp. 173-5, 289-95; Mendoza, *Anuario, 1887,* p. 92; Mendoza, *Memoria, 1903,* pp. 112-15, and chart following p. 130; and *Segundo Censo Nacional* (1895), 3:127, 159.

4. This discussion of stockraising in Mendoza is based on an analysis of data appearing in: Latzina, *L'agriculture,* pp. 289-95; Latzina, *Geografía argentina,* pp. 389-90; Mendoza, *Anuario, 1887,* p. 92; Mendoza, *Memoria, 1903,* p. 126; and *Segundo Censo Nacional* (1895), 3:194, 206, 218, and 230.

5. Calculated from: Bunge, *Los ferrocarriles argentinos,* pp. 129-30; and Scobie, *Revolution on the Pampas,* Table 1.

6. The area devoted to vineyards is based on the department reports for 1887, 1888, 1895, and 1903. These figures will not always coincide with subsequent data used in this chapter for several reasons. Data came from department heads who may or may not have been concerned with accuracy, or from the provincial tax office. In the latter case property tax evasion led to underreporting on the one hand, while on the other, proprietors sometimes overreported to justify receiving more water for irrigation which would allow them to plant more vines. The data for a given year could represent all vines, all hectares above some minimum (0.5 to 1, usually), just those vineyards in production (at least three years old) or a combination of these. There is no way to distinguish which occurred in most years.

   These problems are reflected in the two different totals which appear in one memoria (1903) and in the significant difference in two separate sources for 1914 (55,344 and 70,467 hectares). In the latter case (from the third national census) the figure undoubtedly includes all new plantings. Accordingly, the highest figures for each department in the various reports for a given year were used for this discussion since whether or not the vineyard was mature does not matter in terms of increased area devoted to grape cultivation. Unless otherwise noted, the statistical basis for the analysis of the wine industry between 1885 and 1903 was calculated from: Centro Comercial, Agrícola, e Industrial de Mendoza, *Memoria descriptiva y estadística de la provincia de Mendoza* (Mendoza,

1893), p. 61; Jacinto Alvarez, *Mensaje* (II, 1899), p. 10; Latzina, *L'agriculture*, pp. 173-5; Mendoza, *Anuario, 1887*, p. 90; Mendoza, *Memoria*, 1903, p. 116, and chart following p. 130; and *Segundo Censo Nacional* (1895), 3:139, 183-4.

7. Eusebio Blanco to the Minister of Finance of Mendoza Province, 23 May 1886, Carpeta 42, Documento 173, AHM; and Mendoza, *Memoria, 1903*, chart following p. 164. Blanco was director of the province's statistical office at the time of his report.

8. J. Clark, *Prospecto del tráfico*, pp. 3-10.

9. Provincial Law of 24 November 1884.

10. Mendoza, *Memoria, 1903*, chart following p. 154.

11. "Impuesto al ganado en Chile," *Los Andes*, 28 December 1897, p. 2. The tax went into effect in January, 1898.

12. Luis Galdames, *A History of Chile* (New York, 1964), pp. 405-7.

13. "El ganado argentino," *Los Andes*, 2 February 1901, p. 4.

14. Based on values of poor to high quality cattle as reported in Mendoza, *Memoria, 1903*, p. 127.

15. The discussion of the total value of exports and imports in the Chilean trade is based on: *Registro estadístico de la República Argentina* (formerly, *Anuario estadístico del comercio exterior*), 1898, 1:327, 373; 1899, 1:244, 258; and 1904, 1:373-4. The discussion of both livestock and nonlivestock exports to Chile is based on calculations made from the same sources, for each of the corresponding years between 1885 and 1902. Unfortunately, in no year did the *Registro* report the composition of imports.

16. Calculated from the registry of daily shipments made from the Gran Oeste's stations in Mendoza which the company submitted to the provincial government in 1895. "Resumen de la cantidad de vino y alcohol transpartado (sic) fuera de la provincia de Mendoza durante el ano 1894," Carpeta 76, Documentos 156, 157, 160, and 164.

17. Calculated from Mendoza, *Anuario, 1883*, p. 44; 1906, pp. 23-30, 32-35; *1909*, pp. 252-9; *1910*, pp. 364, 431; *1911*, p. 407; and *Memoria, 1903*, charts following p. 164.

18. Mendoza, *Síntesis de los Anuarios, 1915-1922* (Mendoza, 1923), p. 148. The data on grape prices by year, 1887-1915, also appears in Pedro F. Sabella, *Tratado de geografía general, humana, económica y corográfico de la Provincia de Mendoza* (Mendoza, 1936), p. 278.

19. "Centro viti-vinícola nacional," *Los Andes*, 16 October 1906, p. 3.

20. Elias Villanueva, *Mensaje* (II, 1902), p. 3.

21. Pedro N. Arata, et al., *Investigación vinícola: Informes* (Buenos Aires, 1903), pp. 5-8. Arata was a native Argentine of Italian descent. A specialist in biological chemistry, he taught at the Faculty of Medicine at the University of Buenos Aires, was dean of the Agronomy and Veterinary Institute, director of the Municipal Chemical Office of Buenos Aires. See: Jorge F. Sergi, *Historia de los italianos en la Argentina* (Buenos Aires, 1940), p. 141.

22. A. N. Galanti, *La industri viti-vinícola argentina* (Buenos Aires, 1900), pp. 116-18.

23. See for example: "El porvenir de nuestros vinos," *Los Andes,* 4 February 1887, p. 1; C. de R., "La industria vinícola," *El Economista,* 2:99 (October 21, 1893): 4; Cayetano Gandolfi, "Informe sobre los vinos argentinos en la Exposicion Universal de 1889," *La República Argentina en la Exposición Universal de París de 1889,* ed. Santiago Alcorta (Paris, 1890), pp. 109-11; and Pavolowsky, *La viticultura en la República Argentina,* p. 21. Gandolfi stated that the Argentine wines presented at the Paris exposition suffered from these shortcomings: "Badly elaborated; badly filtered; badly fermented; lack of aroma; generally undefined color; complete lack of distinct classification."

24. "La política y la crisis," *Los Andes,* 5 February 1902, p. 4.

25. Mendoza, *Memoria, 1903,* p. 163.

26. Pedro N. Arata, et al., *Investigación vinícola complementaria de 1904* (Buenos Aires, 1904), p. 5.

27. See for example: Leopoldo Suárez, *Experimentos sobre vinificación* (Buenos Aires, 1907).

28. Mendoza, *Anuario, 1914,* p. 355.

29. Calculated from: Bunge, *Los ferrocarriles argentinos,* pp. 120-21.

30. Scobie, *Revolution on the Pampas,* Table 1.

31. Mendoza, *Anuario, 1911,* p. 63, and *Síntesis de los anuarios, 1915-1922,* p. 13.

32. The analysis of immigrant settlement patterns is based on calculations made from: Mendoza, *Anuario, 1909,* pp. 483, 487, 491; *1910,* p. 16, *1911,* p. 61; *1912,* p. 15; and *1913,* p. 15.

33. Argentina, Departamento General de Inmigración, *La provincia de Mendoza* (Buenos Aires, 1893), p. 16; and *Tercer Censo Nacional* (1914), 3:219.

34. *Segundo Censo Nacional* (1895), 3:183-4; and *Tercer Censo Nacional* (1914), 5:396.

35. Mendoza, *Anuario, 1909,* p. 355.

36. Latzina, *L'agriculture,* p. 373.

37. *Tercer Censo Nacional* (1914), 5:396.

38. The discussion of agriculture between 1903 and 1914 is based on calculations made from: Emilio Lahitte, "Boletín de estadística agrícola del año 1905," *Boletín del Ministerio de Agricultura,* 5:1 (1905): 58; Luis D. Rodríguez, *La Argentina: Descripción de la Capital Federal, provincias, y territorios nacional* (Buenos Aires, 1908), p. 271; Mendoza, *Anuario, 1909,* pp. 364-9; and *1911,* p. 361; and *Tercer Censo Nacional* (1914), 5:915. The data reported by the *Anuario* of 1910 duplicates that which appears in both the provincial census and *Anuario* for 1909.

39. The discussion of stockraising is based on calculations made from: Mendoza, *Memoria, 1903,* p. 126; Provincia de Mendoza, *Censo General, 1909* (Buenos Aires, 1910), pp. 103-9; and *Tercer Censo Nacional* (1914), 6:189-91. The data from the provincial census of 1909, as in the provincial *anuarios* for 1909, 1910, and 1911 is identical to that contained in the national agricultural and stockraising census of 1908.

40. Based on: Mendoza, *Anuario, 1909,* p. 359; and *1914,* p. 205; Mendoza, *Memoria, 1903,* p. 116, and chart following p. 130; and *Tercer Censo Nacional* (1914), 5:929-30.

41. The emphasis on vineyards and wine production in official statistics is exemplified by the failure to record the area devoted to distinct agricultural products. The provincial annual sometimes reported the aggregate data as "Vineyards, Orchards, and Other Crops." See: Mendoza, *Anuario, 1910,* p. 4; *1912,* p. 5; *1913,* p. 5; and *1914,* p. 5.

42. See: Mendoza, *Anuario, 1906,* pp. 23-6, 32-5; *1909,* pp. 252-9; and *1910,* pp. 361, 364, 431.

43. Calculated from: Mendoza, *Anuario, 1910,* p. 361; *1911,* p. 344; *1912,* p. 354; *1913,* p. 344; and *1914,* pp. 208, 218; and *Memoria, 1903,* charts following p. 164.

44. Mendoza, *Anuario, 1909,* p. 373. For the years 1907 and 1908 there was a 2.4 percent and 2.8 percent difference, respectively, between the wine export totals for the first and last six months of each year. In 1907 the difference appeared in the first half-year, and in 1908, in the last half-year.

45. "Resumen," Carpeta 76, Documentos 157, 160, 164, AHM, and Mendoza, *Anuario, 1911,* p. 354.

46. Calculated from Mendoza, *Anuario, 1910,* pp. 361, 364, and 431.

47. Calculated from: Argentina, *Censo Nacional de Agricultura y Ganadería* (Buenos Aires, 1937), pp. xix, xxxvi, 22-7.

Chapter 4

Meeting the Challenge:
Mendoza's Response to the Changing National Economy

Almost from the beginning of their province's era of modern development the mendocinos faced stark realities that converted the high expectations they held into frustration and outrage. The transformational qualities long attributed to iron rails and steam engines, for example, proved mythical. Although the completion of rail links to eastern markets eliminated the restrictive nature of traditional cartage, it also exposed the province to new challenges such as fluctuating freight charges, free trade advocates, the vagaries of distant markets, speculators, and competing interest groups. In short, prosperity seemed possible but development no longer looked quite so inevitable as they once thought.

In response to these new realities local entrepreneurs and government officials changed their practices and policies concerning the provincial economy. At first, progressive members of the oligarchy joined by a few immigrants limited their actions to locally focused measures while they waited for the railroad and market forces to work their influence. While the elite's behavior fulfilled one requirement of initial growth noted earlier--exemplary economic commitment--the mendocinos also exhibited a second orientation pivotal to long-range development. They attempted to maintain an open society and an open economy that would facilitate assimilation and mobility for newly emergent entrepreneurs. As a result, small to moderate scale investors proliferated especially during the second provincial boom when immigration rates soared.

By then the mendocinos had initiated a tenacious defense of the local economy, particularly the wine industry, against perceived threats to their individual and collective success. In abandoning their formerly passive orientation, many entrepreneurs sought to harness the traditional individualism of the province through the formation of voluntary associations. These societies sought to foment and to modernize wine production as well as to organize opposition to taxes, wine falsification, lax customs regulations, and the freight rates set by the railroads. While such measures focused on problems beyond direct local control, the province also suffered from severe internal difficulties especially within the wine industry. Until the eve of World War I, however, attempts to impose order on the sector failed in the face of individualism, outcries against "monopolistic" practices, and the vested interests of speculators and inexperienced producers in search of quick profits.

As implied by the concern over the practices of major producers, several very large bodegas had emerged by the early part of this century. Their continued existence has lent credence to the somewhat popular belief that the industry owes its success to the arrival of European immigrants with sufficient capital to buy large tracts of land or to install high capacity bodegas. This notion exists side by side with the well-known and often expressed pride of the mendocinos in the way in which hard work, initiative, and drive created an "oasis" out of near-desert. It is the latter idea and not the former that comes closest to reflecting historical reality.

As with many of their native mendocino counterparts, even the most important immigrant-owned vineyards and bodegas operating in 1914 had started as minor establishments in the 1880s and 1890s. The growth of those businesses stemmed from the persistent manner in which the foreign-born and native mendocinos reinvested their earnings in grape cultivation and wine production. The leading interests from both groups expressed a desire not only to expand their businesses but also to modernize their operations and to improve the quality of their products. Of course, many producers ignored the example set by their more progressive members and thus contributed to the wine crisis of 1903.

When the province entered a major period of economic growth after 1903, the volume of land transfers hit record highs. Undoubtedly, speculators and major capitalists benefitted from these transactions. But by 1914 the number of small to medium size property owners had increased significantly while large landholders gradually diminished. In similar fashion wine makers installed numerous small bodegas while established producers steadily expanded the capacity of their plants. Mendoza became one of the most important industrial centers in the nation.[1] By 1913 the province held 6 percent of all industrial establishments in the country, had 11 percent of the total capital invested, and accounted for 5 percent of the total value of production.[2] The federal capital and Buenos Aires and Santa Fe provinces with their prosperous flour and meat processing industries based on international export markets dominated the statistics. Outside of these three areas Mendoza far exceeded any other province in capital invested and vied annually with Tucumán for first place in value of production.

Behind this process stood the public policy initiatives of Mendoza's government. If on the pampa ranchers and farmers could respond individually to the opportunities of the 1880s with little governmental intervention, in Mendoza public action had to precede entrepreneurial initiative because of the vital importance of irrigation to agriculture. The relationship of public policy to the private sector, however, went far beyond that mandatory linkage. For example, fiscal policies were drafted to stimulate key sectors of the economy, especially grapegrowing, in their early stages. Protectionist policies of this nature reflected a traditional view of the economic responsibilities of government and extended into a variety of areas supportive of local interests.

The government's approval in 1884 of the Ley de Aguas fulfilled a vital requirement of commercial agriculture in the province.[3] The law protected the river system from abusive exploitation; provided agriculturalists with maximum security; and gave the government the means to promote the incorporation of greater amounts of land into production. Moreover, how the government administered the law was crucial in determining the land tenure system that characterized Mendoza's modern development.

All official attempts to the contrary on the coast, by the turn of the century the humid pampa had come under the control of a few large landowners "to be held for speculation, investment, or prestige--but not to be owned by those who cultivated the land."[4] Powerful interests had subverted the measures adopted by progressive presidents in the 1870s and 80s designed to open the pampa to immigrant farmers. That this would not occur in Mendoza stemmed in part from the direct control of the government over water rights and from the precedents established in the 1880s and 90s.[5] In denying one request for water to irrigate several thousand acres the government observed: ". . . to concede definitive water rights to such a large expanse of land, which would demand for its proper servicing a large part of the water available from the Diamante River [San Rafael], would not be good policy and [at any rate] it is nearly impossible for the petitioner to cultivate such a large area on his own."[6]

Successive administrations maintained this attitude while investing large sums of money in expanding the irrigation capacity of the province's waterways. By 1914 the government had overseen the construction of an extensive and complex irrigation network. At the same time its cautious allocation of resources, the intensive nature of grape cultivation in particular, and a strong tradition of independent farming had provided for an increasing number of small to medium sized producers in all sectors of the rural economy.

Prior to the 1880s Mendoza had numerous self-sufficient farms and ranches.[7] This tradition of the small, independent agriculturalist remained firm throughout Mendoza's development. For example, in 1903 a survey of seven departments found that the largest single wheat farm contained just 90 hectares while more tnan half of the wheat farmers worked 5 hectares or less.[8] According to the 1914 national census Mendoza had over 10,000 landowners. Nearly three-fourths of these owned 50 hectares or less.

The most significant number of small productive units appeared in the wine industry. Between 1883 and 1914 the number of grapegrowers increased from just under 1,500 to more than 6,000. During the same period the amount of land planted with grapevines rose from 2,700 hectares to over 70,000 hectares. In 1883 only 33 growers held 10 hectares or more; in 1914, 85 percent of the grape cultivators held less than 25 hectares each. As a group, the viticulturalists represented 61 percent of all landowners in the province.[9]

The installation of winemaking facilities (bodegas) exhibited a similar pattern. Between 1895 and 1914 the number of bodegas in the province rose from 433 to 1507 while their capital worth increased from 7,000,000 $m/n to 149,000,000 $m/n.[10] Nearly three-fifths of the bodegas registered in 1912 had a capacity of 500 hls. or less. Just 10 percent made 5,000 hls. or more. A cross check of the list of winemakers showed that only eight owned more than one bodega.[11] With rare exceptions even the largest establishments began through the efforts of entrepreneurs with only modest sums of money.

Although the province developed rapidly, cheap cultivable land available in small units remained abundant. Of course, in a booming economy entrepreneurs with a sizeable financial base could become rich, especially if they succeeded in land speculation. Once cultivated with grain crops or planted in vines, the land became very valuable. But even in the core departments cultivable land sold at modest prices. This contributed to a growing subdivision of property while the market price of developed tracts stimulated a rush to plant vineyards.

After 1900 with the initiation of massive immigration, the extension of the Gran Oeste Railroad to San Rafael, and the resurgence of wine consumption on the coast, the volume of land sales hit unprecedented levels. During a ten-year period (1902-11) over 23 million hectares of land were sold, more than in any other province in the country.[12] In 1905 land sales reached a record high of nearly 5,600,000 hectares valued at just under 22,000,000 $m/n. In 1910 land transfers in Mendoza represented 26 percent of the national total. Moreover, the low percentage of sales that carried mortgages indicates that a significant amount of real capital circulated in the province. In the record year 1905, 6 percent of the area sold and 17 percent of its value was mortgaged. For the decade 1902-11 mortgages represented 17 percent of the total land transferred and 34 percent of its value.

If the subdivision of property and the spread of small production units supported the province's development, they also generated serious problems. The inexperienced and the unskilled could' plant vines and make wine as easily as those practiced in modern techniques. Producers in search of quick profits sacrificed quality for quantity. By the turn of the century a near anarchic situation plagued the wine industry. For three years (1901-03) Mendoza's main industry endured a turbulent recession that affected mainly grape growers. The average selling price of grapes suffered a precipitous drop between 1900 and 1901 and the planting of vineyards came to a halt.[13]

The immediate cause of the crisis seemed to lie in the relationship between supply, demand, and productive capacities. Between 1899 and 1902 wine exports stabilized after twelve years of accelerated expansion. In part, this reflected a leveling off of national consumption. Production in Mendoza, nevertheless, increased by more than 50 percent.[14]

During the era of seemingly unlimited expansion in wine production and exportation growers planted vines at an average rate of 1,400 hectares per year. Between 1891 and 1898 the total area of vineyards increased at least 10,000 hectares. By 1901 the entire amount had begun to bear fruit, with nearly 60 percent in full production.[15] The winemakers could not absorb the record harvests, and the selling price of grapes fell as growers exported the fruit in unprecedented amounts.[16] With little capital the small producers who could not endure even a temporary drop in prices emptied their bodegas as fast as possible. Stories spread of wholesale wine falsification, the rejection of Mendoza's wines by consumers on the coast, conspiracies by vested interests in Buenos Aires, and the imminent bankruptcy of the province.[17]

A commercial panic started that clouded over the real financial and economic stability of the province. The productive capacity of grape cultivation had increased with the abundant yield of new vineyards. In 1902 the cereal harvests promised to be very good; businesses operated smoothly, if less profitably compared to other years; debtors consistently met their obligations; and Mendoza's exports sold well in both coastal and interior markets. [18]

As consumer demand picked up on the coast under the influence of a new era of massive immigration, these realities erased the crisis of confidence, and Mendoza's economy recovered rapidly. [19] Even before the national commission that had studied the crisis completed its report, the selling price of grapes had risen and the setting out of vines had resumed its normal rate. By 1905 grapes sold at their highest price in ten years. [20]

The position of small producers in the crisis indicates the emergence of a division of production in Mendoza's wine industry that would eventually cause more serious problems later in the century. As the making of wine and its commercialization became more sophisticated, the cost of building and maintaining large bodegas increased. Concurrently, large bodegas found that their vineyards did not supply their needs and that their production did not fill their purchase orders. In addition, the many small vineyards, operating with little capital, either did not or could not establish bodegas. As a result, Mendoza had bodegas with and without vineyards, and conversely, viticulturalists with and without bodegas.

By the end of the province's pre-World War I development this structure had placed significant power in the hands of the largest winemakers. Small and medium bodegas began to sell their wines to the big producers, who had near-control over the marketing process. Eventually this system gave a few bodegas the power to dictate prices. But in 1910, for example, only 4 percent of the wine made in Mendoza was sold from one bodega to another. [21] Moreover, the activities of the founders of a commodities exchange for wine in 1911 indicate the leading producers did not attempt to monopolize the industry for their own benefit. At any rate, the structure of the wine industry in 1903 had not become sufficiently sophisticated to have permitted conspiratorial practices to cause the crisis.

Regardless of its immediate origin and its short duration, the crisis served to focus attention on long-standing problems in the wine industry and to stimulate progressive interests to redouble their efforts in defense of Mendoza's economy. To provide themselves with an organized means through which to channel their activities, the mendocinos formed voluntary associations. These groups served to foment the modernization of the wine industry and to organize defensive measures against any threats to Mendoza's development. Often, they worked in concert with the provincial government.

The need for cooperation between the public and private sectors became particularly apparent during the national financial crisis of the 1890s. By that time the escalating cost of public works projects, like building a 400,000 $m/n master dam on the Mendoza River, had severely strained provincial revenues. [22] To raise money the government placed taxes on mature vineyards and on wine exported from the province. [23] These measures provided the province with a substantial revenue base and between 1896 and 1914 the wine industry's contribution to local revenue escalated from 23 percent to 66 percent. [24]

With the health of the provincial treasury increasingly dependent on the wine sector perceived threats from external interests generated a vigorous response from both the public and private sectors. During the 1890s local concern became intense when the national government started to eye the expanding wine industry as a likely target for taxation. Lobbying efforts were led by both provincial officials and the members of the *Centro Comercial, Agrícola e Industrial,* the province's oldest and most comprehensive voluntary association.

In general, the Centro's activities ranged from the diffusion of information about Mendoza to the arbitration of complaints against the Gran Oeste Railroad. Under the auspices of the provincial government the Centro published in 1893 a descriptive and statistical analysis of Mendoza. The extensive publication (131 pages) not only presented technical information but also provided propaganda to attract investors and immigrants. It described the proper method for planting grapevines and the costs of cultivating a variety of crops. Charts appeared on workers' salaries, rents, construction costs, and the prices of agricultural equipment. The Centro emphasized the ample opportunities for immigrants to become property owners, and it supported the claim with lists of foreign-born businessmen, landholders, and winemakers. [25]

During the 1890s the Centro kept constant pressure on the Gran Oeste Argentino to improve its service and to lower its freight rates. The appeals for reduced shipping charges usually took the form of detailed petitions to the national government. [26] If these petitions failed, the Centro would reinforce their content with additional arguments and resubmit the document. [27] On at least one occasion the Centro collected money from its members to send a lobbyist to Buenos Aires in support of its demands. [28] When the Gran Oeste's general manager attempted to systematize claims procedures with the mendocinos, he worked through the directorate of the Centro. [29]

The association's most important activities, however, came in the face of three threats to Mendoza's prosperity that the financial crisis of the 1890s generated: national taxation, the rising sales of falsified wines, and an antiprotectionist campaign. For seven years the Centro spearheaded a successful attempt to prevent national taxation of true wine. Congress approved a small impost in 1898, but under pressure from the association, provincial officials, and wine interests, it lowered the tax in 1899 and then rescinded the law the following year. [30]

Perhaps of a greater threat to Mendoza's economy than national taxation was imported wine and artificial wine. Frequently, coastal interests imported wine of a high alcoholic content which they then watered down, colored, and sweetened for sale. Often they attached labels to the bottles indicating that they were from Mendoza or San Juan, thus contributing to a poor reputation for Cuyo's products. [31] The early 1890s brought a double blow to both legitimate importers and falsifiers. First, the tariff on common wine was raised to 80 percent. [32] Then the gold premium sharply escalated the cost of importing wine and thus the cost of using the latter to make spurious wines. By the middle of the decade a battle broke out at the national level that took the form of a classic free trade versus protectionism debate. The Centro's multifaceted efforts in the face of these combined threats included research on the extent of falsification, petitions, an analysis of imported wines, and requests for support from other societies.

Securing the passage of legislation to impede the sale of artificial wine presented the least difficulties. After its victory against a wine tax in 1892, the Centro Comercial submitted petitions in favor of a strong impost on falsified wine.[33] The members of the association supported their demands with the results of an investigation into the quantity of artificial wine made and sold in the country.[34] Rufino Cubillos, president of the Centro, sent a copy of their investigation, the projects submitted to Congress and a supporting letter to the Sociedad Rural to obtain the society's assistance.[35] When Congress approved a pure wine law and levied a tax on falsified wines in October 1893, all efforts turned to the question of imports.[36]

The mendocinos faced a united front from free trade advocates, Spanish merchants, and some national legislators. In response, the members of the Centro Comercial composed a sophisticated comprehensive treatise intended to dismantle the opposition's case point by point.[37] The contents of their exposition demonstrate an in-depth knowledge of economic theory and history, of the works of contemporary oenologists and specialists, and of the state of the wine industries in other producing countries. This expertise supported the Centro's strong defense of Mendoza's interests, a defense which itself reflects the progressive pioneer spirit that motivated the mendocinos.

With the Centro Comercial leading the way Mendoza succeeded in preventing passage of the new regulations, but the apparent need for constant vigilance of Mendoza's wine interests led to the formation of a separate association, the Centro Vitivinícola Argentino (Argentine Wine Production Center). With offices in Buenos Aires the Centro Vitivinícola would defend and advance Mendoza's wine industry before national, provincial, and municipal authorities; disseminate information on modern techniques; study new inventions and other improvements beneficial to the industry; and maintain contact with similar associations in other provinces.[38] Most, if not all, of the Centro Vitivinícola's members also belonged to the Centro Comercial, which continued to defend the wine industry.

The new association began its activities in the midst of the conflict over foreign wines. Its members worked to unite the interior provinces behind a protectionist campaign. They sent circulars to eight provincial governors asking that each one send a delegate to Buenos Aires, where a group would coordinate efforts on behalf of both the sugar and wine industries. Only Córdoba refused to cooperate with the Centro Vitivinícola's plans.[39]

The association kept constant pressure on the national government to favor the wine industry. In 1895 the group petitioned Congress to free from customs duties all material imported for use in grape and wine production.[40] Any attempt to tax wine generated an immediate strong response often carried out with the complementary action of the Centro Comercial.[41] The use of raisins to make spurious wines brought petitions from the Centro Vitivinícola first to place a heavy duty on imported raisins and then to outlaw the use of anything but fresh grapes to produce wine.[42]

In 1905 the Society of Grocers in Buenos Aires went on strike and petitioned Congress to modify a law on the sale of falsified wine. The wine association protested vigorously, and the government rejected the grocers' demands. [43]

The service and freight charges of the Gran Oeste Railroad came under close scrutiny. In 1895 the Centro Comercial sought the cooperation of the wine society in its attempt to persuade the railroad not to raise its charges. [44] When the wine crisis hit grape producers they won a series of rebates from the company. [45] Concern over the proper construction of boxcars for wine shipments led to a request by the Centro Vitivinícola that the railroad provide for the proper ventilation of its cars. [46]

When the crisis of 1902-03 hit, the wine industry's leading producers sought the creation of a more comprehensive association. With the support of the provincial government they established the Centro Vitivinícola de Mendoza in late 1904. A few months later these same interests formed a new national organization based in Buenos Aires, the Centro Vitivinícola Nacional, with the Mendoza society merged into it. [47] As previous organizations had done these two groups defended the province against external threats and supported modernization. The Centros lobbied successfully, for example, with the railroads in 1905 for a reduction in freight rates for the return of empty casks to producers. In 1906 the provincial Centro played a key role in quickly and amicably mediating a strike against the Gran Oeste Railroad. [48]

While the province's susceptibility to outside forces had justified such organized measures in the view of most mendocinos the crisis of 1902-03 also convinced several producers of the need for an internal association to impose order on the wine industry itself. Their idea, however, conjured up images of monopoly control and of wine trusts run by powerful entrepreneurs. [49] The controversy produced a shake-up in the provincial and national Centros when in 1907 supporters of regulation established the Bolsa Vitivinícola y Comercial, a commodities exchange for grapes and wine. [50] Critics condemned the Bolsa as a union of large-scale winemakers that ignored the interests of the growers. In 1908 the association won passage of a provincial law forbidding the exportation of wine grapes. [51] Their action, however, probably prevented the reduction of Mendoza to solely a grape producing province through the transfer of wine processing to Buenos Aires and other major consumer centers.

For three years the members of the Bolsa tried to expand their organization into an all inclusive association of grape and wine producers. They achieved their goal in 1911 with the foundation of the *Sociedad de Vitivinicultores de Mendoza* (The Society of Grape and Wine Producers of Mendoza). According to its charter, the Sociedad would serve as a center for all transactions and operations related to the wine industry. It would establish cooperatives to make purchases for its members in volume and thus reduce unit costs. Arbitration boards would handle disputes that might arise between producers. In general, the Sociedad would represent the industry's interests before all political, financial, commercial, and transportation entities; promote modern techniques; and watch over the quality of production through the use of inspectors and its own laboratories. [52]

In his address to the organizational meeting of the Sociedad, Leopoldo Suárez indirectly attributed the failure of previous attempts to form the association to the individualistic drive and the faith in personal achievement that characterized the mendocinos.[53] Indeed, a tradition of personal advancement based on one's own efforts contributed to the preservation of a competitive economy that provided for the mutual participation of small, medium, and large scale producers. This tradition, reinforced by the progressive activities of both native and immigrant leaders in the wine industry, led to a collective effort to develop Mendoza.

The establishment and operation of voluntary associations represented the joint efforts of entrepreneurs from all levels of the economy. The Centro Comercial, Agrícola e Industrial included members of traditional mendocino families (Civit, González, Godoy, Nanclares) and immigrants (Tomba, Escorihuela, Falco, Sarramea). Its varied membership covered professionals like newspaper editor Adolfo Calle and agronomist-educator José R. Ponce, in addition to an array of businessmen, wine producers, agriculturalists, stockraisers, and politicians. The Centro's president owned a small vineyard of 30 hectares.[54] Individual grape producers who signed the declaration of principles for the Centro Vitivinícola owned as few as 10 hectares and as many as 300 hectares of vineyards.[55] The capacity of bodegas operated by the organizers of the Sociedad de Vitivinicultores ranged from 4,000 hls. to 260,000 hls.[56]

In the forefront of every association appeared a select group of entrepreneurs who came from the pioneering core of the industry. Popular tradition ascribes the modern development of the wine industry to Italian and Spanish immigrants. These include Domingo Tomba, Juan Giol, Miguel Escorihuela, Pascual Tosso, Balbino Arizu, and many others. But native-born mendocinos operated on a par with their immigrant associates. The industry's leading producers included Honorio Barraquero, Tiburcio Benegas, Elías Villanueva, Carlos González, and Melitón Arroyo among others.[57]

Collectively, they symbolized the kind of personal drive and entrepreneurial activities that generally characterized the mendocinos. Their search for ways to modernize the wine industry ranged from the practical to the exotic. One investor tried to apply the petroleum technology of the United States and Russia to the transportation of wine. He planned to build a pipeline from Mendoza to Buenos Aires with large bodegas at each end.[58] Several years later one of Mendoza's largest producers, Juan Giol, installed a two-mile long pipeline to conduct wine between his bodegas.[59]

The serious attention given by Los Andes to the project for a cross-country pipeline reflects the open-minded concern for modernization that many mendocinos held. This concern, exercised in an environment that traditionally rewarded initiative, contributed significantly to the economic growth of the province. The mendocinos studied new techniques in grape cultivation and winemaking, installed modern machinery in their bodegas, experimented with a wide variety of vines, and above all, repeatedly reinvested their profits in the industry to promote its development. As a publication of the Centro Vitivinícola Nacional put it: "Different features certainly exist between the families of note in this region of the country and those on the coast. The names respected for the wealth and social position they represent come from the great hacienda owners over there. In Cuyo, they are agriculturalists, vintners preferably."[60] The emphasis in Mendoza, the anonymous writer commented, was on one's productivity and thus, one's contribution to the collective wealth of the province, not on the acquisition of empty titles representing professions (law and medicine) that one will never pursue.[61]

To protect and to improve the position of the province within the national economy the mendocinos formed voluntary associations. These groups defended Mendoza against unfair customs regulations, the activities of wine falsifiers, the policies of the railroads, and repeated national government attempts to tax wine. They used a variety of methods to achieve their goals: petitions to Congress, an organized protectionist campaign, representatives in Buenos Aires, and committees that met with railroad and provincial government officials.

The policies, practices, and attitudes of the local entrepreneurs reflected a twofold reaction to the problems of Mendoza's modern development. Before 1885 they and local public officials had concentrated their activities on the internal elements of development such as irrigation and the modernization of grape cultivation and wine production. After 1885 it became increasingly necessary to take a much more active stance against perceived external threats to Mendoza's prosperity.

The provincial government in particular took action during the 1890s when multiple forces worked against local development. For example, in 1898 the provincial legislature passed a sweeping resolution that condemned the idea of a federal tax on wine and lobbyists in Buenos Aires successfully pressured the national minister of finance into opposing Congress's tax proposal.[62] Two years later the province provided for the transfer of 2,000 $m/n monthly from the revenue its own wine tax generated for the support and defense of the industry and to underwrite the expenses of the Centro Vitivinícola in Buenos Aires.[63] In 1897 the local government had created a special commission to help direct the defense of the wine industry.[64]

The revenues that accrued to the province from its wine and vineyard taxes were reinvested by the government in areas like irrigation, roads, education, public relations, and common interest lobbying. In the late 1880s the government successfully negotiated the transfer of the national agronomy school to provincial control. It then passed a series of measures to reform the curriculum, improve its facilities and staffing, and to expand its ability to experiment with livestock strains and crops. By 1903 the institution had at least twenty-eight students and seven professors.[65]

The government's support for public education in general and its direct involvement in agricultural and viticultural studies in particular typified the local elite's emphasis on practical or technical knowledge as a necessary component of Mendoza's economic success. Technical knowledge could be imparted through formal education but it also could be both expressed and learned at expositions. The government's role was to sponsor both types of activities and, at times, to underwrite the cost of sending representatives to fairs to study the latest agricultural techniques. The government took an active position on such matters because the accumulation of practical knowledge benefited the common welfare of the mendocinos. Thus, for example, the province not only sponsored its own exposition at the time of the railroad's inauguration in 1885, it also participated in the Sociedad rural fairs in Buenos Aires, and the Universal Exposition in Paris in 1889. When the first National Congress on Commerce and Industry met in Córdoba in 1911 they selected Mendoza as the site of the second congress, to meet two years later. [66]

In making their decision the delegates recognized that Mendoza's economic success had given the province a prominent position within the nation. To arrive at that position the mendocinos had to confront a number of challenges stemming from the realities of Argentina's own growth and its integration into an expanding international economy. Particularly crucial for the province were the echoes of the international financial crisis of the 1890s that magnified old conflicts and structural contradictions. This was especially the case for the pressures that the crisis brought to bear on domestic industries, and the national treasury.

The mendocinos responded by drawing upon tradition, closing ranks, and turning "outward" to defend their economy vigorously before national officials, free trade advocates, coastal interests, speculators, and the railroads. Within the province public policy and private entrepreneurship continued to fulfill the roles they had played since long before the railroad's arrival and the pampa's rapid development. Obviously, the actions of the mendocinos as private citizens and public officials do not by themselves account for the province's economic successes before World War I. But it is with reason that people in Buenos Aires speak in admiring fashion of the mendocinos as being "muy bravos;" it is with reason that Mendoza has been known as "La tierra del sol y de buen vino," and as "La perla andina;" and it is with reason that the mendocinos themselves speak of their province in such prideful terms as an oasis they created. From their experiences there is much to be learned about domestic development under conditions of external dependency.

Endnotes for Chapter 4

1. Arata, *Investigación vinícola,* p. 219; and Luis D. Rodríguez, *La Argentina en el año 1912* (Buenos Aires, 1912), p. 308.

2. Adolfo Dorfman, *Historia de la industria argentina* (Buenos Aires, 1970), p. 313.

3. Ley de Aguas (November 24, 1884).

4. Scobie, *Revolution on the Pampas,* p. 118.

5. Provincial Decree of 20 September 1887; Jacinto Alvarez, *Mensaje* (I, 1899), pp. 10-11; Provincial Law No. 35 (1897); and Provincial Law No. 142 (1899).

6. Provincial Decrees of 12 February and 24 August 1885.

7. C. Villanueva, *El litoral y el interior,* p. 130.

8. Mendoza, *Memoria, 1903,* chart following p. 130.

9. Calculated from: Mendoza, *Padrón de viñas,* p. 63; *Segundo Censo Nacional* (1895), 3:183-4; Mendoza, *Memoria, 1903, p.* 115; and *Tercer Censo Nacional* (1914), 5:207, 929-30.

10. Calculated from: Departamento General de Inmigración, *La Provincia de Mendoza,* p. 18; *Segundo Censo Nacional* (1895), 3:326; Mendoza, *Anuario, 1909,* pp. 382-3; and *Tercer Censo Nacional* (1914), 7:152.

11. Rodríguez, *1912,* pp. 309-11.

12. Lahitte, *Informes y Estudios,* 2:211; 3:14, 20; and 5:62-3.

13. Mendoza, *Síntesis de los Anuarios,* 1915-22, p. 148.

14. Arata, Investigación vinícola, p. 219.

15. Calculated from: Mendoza, *Síntesis de los Anuarios, 1915-22,* p. 148. Because of faulty reporting these are most probably minimal figures.

16. Elias Villanueva, *Mensaje* (II, 1902), p. 27-8; and Mendoza, *Memoria, 1903,* charts following p. 164. The export figures for 1902 and 1903 are for the first six months only of each year; but the harvest of grapes occurs during this period.

17. "La crisis actual," *Los Andes,* 9 February 1902, p. 4; "Los vinos," *Los Andes,* 6 June, p. 4; "La crisis vinícola," *Los Andes,* 20 January 1903, pp. 4-5; and "La crisis del vino," *Los Andes,* 22 April 1903, pp. 4-5.

18. "La política y la crisis," *Los Andes,* 5 February 1902, p. 4.

19. Between 1903 and 1904 net immigration to Argentina increased from 37,900 to 94,500. Over the next five years net immigration averaged 150,000 new arrivals per year. Based on Scobie, *Revolution on the Pampas,* Table 1.

20. Mendoza, *Síntesis de los Anuarios, 1915-1922,* p. 148.

21. Calculated from: Rodríguez, *La Argentina,* 1912, p. 309. In the late 1940s the province bought the largest bodega in Mendoza (Giol) and used the establishment to set quasi-official prices for wine and grapes.

22. Cesar Cippoletti, *Memoria* (1894), Carpeta C 525, Documento 5, AHM; Emilio R. Cano, *Sanaemiento de la Provincia de Mendoza* (Buenos Aires, 1897), p. 53; and Newton, *Diccionario biográfico,* s. v. "Cippoletti, Cesar." Cippoletti executed a number of other works in other provinces before he returned to his native Italy. In late 1907 he was contracted to return to Argentina but died en route on the high seas in January 1908.

23. Provincial Laws of 20 September 1881, 24 December 1889, 22 May 1891, 3 August 1894, 1 April 1895, 3 October 1895; Provincial Laws No. 1 (1896), No. 255 (1902), and No. 348 (1905); and Provincial Decree of 1 April 1895. For related material see: "Datos estadísticos," *Los Andes,* 17 October 1890, p. 1; "Cobro de impuestos a las viñas," *Los Andes,* 4 August 1892, p. 1; and "Impuesto al vino," *Los Andes,* 21 April 1909, p. 5.

24. Lahitte, *Informes y Estudios,* 3:15.

25. Centro Comercial, *Memoria, 1893.*

26. See for example: "La cuestión tarifas," *Los Andes,* 13 July 1890, p. 1; "Las tarifas de los ferrocarriles," *Los Andes,* 1 September 1892, p. 1; and "Mendoza y el Gran Oeste," *Los Andes,* 24 December 1898, p. 2.

27. "Tarífas ferroviárias," *Los Andes,* 9 March 1894, p. 1.

28. "Tarífas del Gran Oeste," *Los Andes,* 14 January 1892, p. 1.

29. "Mendoza," *RRP,* 9 April 1892, p. 11.

30. "Impuesto a los vinos," *Los Andes,* 27 July 1892, p. 2. Centro Comercial, Agrícola, e Industrial, *Solicitud que los bodegueros y viñateros de la Provincia de Mendoza elevan al Honorable Congreso de la Nación, pidiendo la no aceptación del impuesto de 2 centavos por cada litro de vino nacional* (Mendoza, 1897). Dorfman, *Historia de la industria,* cuadro no. 5.

31. Pavlowsky, *La industria vitivinícola,* pp. 29-30.

32. Latzina, *Estadística retrospectiva* (1905), chart on p. 176. The data in the following paragraph is drawn from this same source.

33. "El impuesto a los vinos," *Los Andes,* 25 October 1892, p. 1.

34. "Vitivinicultura," *Los Andes,* 14 September 1899, pp. 4-5.

35. The letter appeared in *Los Andes* under the title, "La cuestión vinos," 25 October 1893, p. 1.

36. National Law No. 3957 (1893), and "La industria vinícola," *Los Andes,* 28 October 1893, p. 1.

37. Centro Comercial, Agrícola, e Industrial, *Exposición presentada a los Señores Diputados y Senadores al H. Congreso Nacional sobre la importancia de la industria vitivinícola* (Mendoza, 1894).

38. "Centro Viti-viniclo [sic]," *Los Andes,* 1 June 1894, p. 1.

39. "La campaña porteccionista," *Los Andes,* 18 July 1894, p. 1.

40. Centro Vitivinícola Argentino, *Petición al Honorable Congreso de la Nación con motivo del projecto de Ley de Aduanas* (Buenos Aires, 1895).

41. See for example: "El impuesto al [sic] los vinos," *Los Andes,* 19 September 1897, p. 2; and Centro Vitivinícola Argentino, *Petición al H. Congreso de la Nación: Modificaciones de la Ley de Impuestos Internos* (Buenos Aires, 1896).

42. Centro Vitivinícola, *Petición* (1895); and "La solicitud de los vinicultores," *Los Andes,* 29 May 1902, p. 5.

43. "La ley de vinos," *Los Andes,* 24 May 1905, p. 4; "La ley de vinos," *Los Andes,* 3 June 1905, p. 4; and Centro de Almaceneros, *La nueva Ley de Vinos: Solicitudes presentadas. . .a los poderes públicos pidiendo su derogación o reforma* (Buenos Aires, 1905).

44. "Las tarifas del Gran Oeste," *Los Andes,* 10 September 1895, p. 1.

45. "La exportación de uva," *Los Andes,* 14 February 1903, p. 6.

46. "Trasporte de vinos," *Los Andes,* 15 January 1898, p. 2.

47. Centro Vitivinícola Nacional, *La vitivincultura Argentina en 1910* (Buenos Aires, 1910), p. xxxii.

48. Ibid., pp. xxxii-xxxiii.

49. See for example: "La liga de bodegueros," *Los Andes,* 15 February 1902, p. 4; and "El trust vinicola," *Los Andes,* 18 July 1902, pp. 4-5.

50. "Bolsa Vitivinícola," *Los Andes,* 29 August 1907, p. 4; and Centro Vitivinícola Nacional, *La vitivinicultura,* p. xxxiii.

51. "La adulteración de los vinos," *Los Andes,* 5 April 1908, p. 4; and "La Bolsa Vitivinícola," *Los Andes,* 30 January 1908, p. 4.

52. The Sociedad's constitution appears in "La unión gremial entre viñateros y bodegueros de Mendoza," *La Viticultura Argentina,* 2d yr., nos. 9, 10, 11 (January, February, and March 1911), pp. 160-9.

53. "La unión gremial," p. 155.

54. Based on the names appearing at the end of Centro Comercial, *Solicitud,* pp. 7-8.

55. A partial list of signees appears in: "Centro viti-vinícola," *Los Andes,* 1 June 1894, p. 31.

56. An incomplete list of organizers appears in: "La unión gremial," pp. 169-70.

57. William J. Fleming, "The Cultural Determinants of Entrepreneurship and Economic Development: A Case Study of Mendoza Province, Argentina, 1861-1914," *Journal of Economic History* 39:1 (March 1979):218-20.

58. "Transporte de vinos," *Los Andes,* 1 June 1897, p. 2.

59. Provincial Decree of 16 November 1911.

60. Centro Vitivinícola Nacional, *La vitivinicultura en 1910,* p. 132.

61. Ibid., p. 146.

62. Provincial Resolution of 26 July 1892; and "El impuesto a los vinos," *Los Andes,* 25 October 1892, p. 1.

63. Provincial Law of 3 August 1894.

64. Provincial Decree of 15 October 1897.

65. Provincial Decrees of 21 December 1886, 20 June 1887, 6 July 1887, 1 September 1887, and 1 May 1889; Provincial Resolution of 1 May 1888; and Mendoza, *Memoria, 1903,* p. 97.

66. Provincial Decrees of 13 Nobember 1885, 16 September 1887, 6 September 1888, and 9 May 1889; and Mendoza, *Memoria del Segundo Congreso de Comercio e Industrias* (Mendoza, 1914), p. 13.

Chapter 5

Speculations on Dependency and
Tradition in a Developing Economy

By the end of Mendoza's early modern economic growth the strength
of the province's export economy revolved around the wine
industry. The remarkable success of viticulture over a few decades
had provided for a high level of general prosperity which in turn
fed a continually diversified internal economy not very different in
composition, with the singularly important exception of wine, from
its pre-railroad characteristics. The strength of the wine industry
seemed to oscillate with that of the coastal agro-export industry.
The latter responded to international market, political, and economic
factors often reflective of a dependency relationship.

Under the worst circumstances, the international connection
could place the interests of one vital element of a regionally based
economy in opposition to another by creating a financial dilemma
with no apparent solution outside of a change in the international
conditions themselves. Alternatively, the same or similar
international circumstances could threaten crucial productive sectors
of the regionally-based economy by juxtaposing powerful national
interests tied to foreign trade with those of a region linked to
domestic commerce. This conflict developed for Mendoza's wine
industry over the issues of protective tariffs, falsification, and
internal taxes.

Under the best circumstances the international-national-regional
continuum offered many benefits to the country but restricted most
of them to a geographically limited area. The rapid growth of
Argentina's agro-export sector injected a significant amount of
dynamism into Argentina's economy. Coupled with unprecedented
immigration and large-scale investment in infrastructure the pampa's
development provided broad opportunities to other agriculturalists,
commercialists, and industrialists. The concentration of agriculture
and stockraising in the same region containing the nation's capital,
its main ports and cities, and much of the growing population
combined with certain aspects of domestic politics, international
diplomacy, and foreign trade to restrict the range of real
opportunity. Thus, much of the activity behind the impressive
national growth statistics registered between 1880 and 1914 occurred
on the pampa and the littoral, especially in Buenos Aires province
and city.

For interests located outside of this dynamic core the avenues for growth were few; and the farther away the fewer they were. Nevertheless, sufficient opportunity existed to permit a province like Mendoza, with a marketable resource like wine, to integrate into the emerging national economy and to experience a level of prosperity proportionate to that of the littoral. The province's comparative advantage in wine production attracted protective tariff policies and a railroad link to the coast. There, the swelling population fueled the viticultural sector of the provincial economy which then expanded rapidly, attracting immigrants on a large scale. Soon, with two-thirds of Mendoza's principal export heading for a single region if the coastal economy either stalled or declined the provincial economy necessarily did the same. Between 1880 and 1914 the provincial and national economies worked virtually in tandem so that they share the same general description of those years as two periods of rapid economic growth separated by a financial crisis. The dependency related continuum seemed to exercise its influence under both the "worst" and the "best" circumstances.

Many statistical facets of Mendoza's economic growth presented in this case study lend credence to the general schema of interior-coastal relationships drawn in the preceding paragraphs. However, a closer examination of the events and actions behind the figures suggests the presence of many more nebulous lines in the schema than appear at first glance. Those "events and actions" which took place at the provincial end of the relationship indicate the need to qualify our ideas about the position of the interior within the export-oriented national economy, the discriminatory grip of the latter on the former, and the role of the national government in the entire process.

The dependency related schema outlined in Chapter 1 holds generally as a description of the basic economic and political relationships that had evolved by the end of Argentina's early modern development, and its bold brush strokes accurately represent the borders of economic opportunity during those years. However, the "borders" may be far wider and the comprehensiveness of the schema as an explanation of what actually took place far narrower than popularly supposed. Ultimately, the basic factors behind the forces and decisions specific to the provincial arena point to the critical role tradition played in Mendoza's growth, and are highly suggestive of a generally applicable connection between traditional culture and economic development. They also indicate that the view from the interior significantly improves the often hazy images of the course of Argentina's economic history during the late nineteenth and early twentieth centuries that we have obtained from purely coastal, national vantagepoints.

The developmental elite which assumed power in 1861 presided over an economy based on commercial agriculture and closely linked with transandine trade. In an era of oxcart and mule-train transportation eastward commerce had been minimal. They also were aware of the viticultural potential of the region. Although they attempted to ship wine to coastal markets, under the traditional forms of cartage wine could and often did turn to vinegar before it arrived there. They anticipated that a railroad link would both open up eastward commerce for many of their traditional products and create a whole new avenue of commerce by making viticulture profitable. They further anticipated that eastward commerce would focus on littoral markets, but not to the exclusion of trade with other regions. They anticipated few of the complications that they encountered.

The developmental elite emphasized technological progress and applied science as crucial to the province's future. They modernized the main elements of the provincial economy and provided for the dissemination of technical and practical knowledge to the broad base of the population. In their roles as government officials they promoted the modernization of agriculture, viticulture, irrigation, and transportation. They built and supported schools and libraries, extended financial aid to poor students, brought specialists in from Europe, participated in expositions, supported an agricultural station, and planned their own fair to coincide with the railroad's inauguration.

As private citizens the developmental elite pursued parallel actions. They studied and exchanged the latest techniques used in Europe and brought specialists to the province to help them modernize their businesses. They experimented with new strains of plants and winemaking techniques. They displayed their products at exhibitions and reinvested their money in further modernizing and expanding their operations. Their actions cut across the economy and included agriculture, stockraising, mining, commerce, and viticulture.

However, serious problems which would periodically plague the province had already begun to appear. Although the progressive elite pursued developmental rather than speculative investment patterns and emphasized the benefits of appropriate technology, they were not necessarily seconded in their efforts by other mendocinos. Abuse of what passed for an irrigation system was widespread and it took years to get a comprehensive water law passed. The first attempts to stimulate viticulture and growing of fruit and walnuts failed to generate a positive response from other than members of the progressive elite. With the potential of viticulture looking stronger toward the beginning of the 1880s investors rushed into the sector in pursuit of profits but with little attention to quality or modern technques.

The government's reaction to increasing competition from agricultural development around Mendoza's traditional export markets in the late 1870s was typically focused on modernization and technical education to enhance the province's competitive edge; but it was also overly optimistic about the power of the two. By the early 1880s Mendoza began to experience the negative effects which would accompany the growth of an externally dependent agro-export economy on the coast. Nevertheless, the opportunities which the beneficial effects of a dependent national economy brought permitted the province to move into its first modern economic boom. Accelerated growth glossed over many of the internal problems and the structural difficulties of integrating into an expanding national economy which Mendoza had already experienced. Most of them would reappear at the end of the first boom.

What happened to the provincial economy during the 1880s seemed to confirm most of the mendocinos' early assumptions. Transandine commerce slumped periodically but generally expanded and eventually reached record highs. Eastward commerce picked up dramatically with national expansion although several traditional candidates for export faded in the face of agricultural growth elsewhere in the country. However, those products did not diminish in production; they expanded as a result of rising internal demand generated by the province's overall development. The irrigation system spread, thousands of hectares came under cultivation, the viticultural sector grew rapidly, capital formation increased, and commerce prospered. Although the wine industry suffered from the failure of bodega capacities to keep pace with increased grape supplies and from a myriad of ill-conceived practices in winemaking itself, the developmental elite felt that education and the manifest superiority of modern techniques would eventually overcome these weaknesses.

Then an international financial crisis hit which carried far more serious dangers for the local economy than the relatively simple matter of resistance to change. As all parties scrambled to protect themselves and to advance their interests the mendocinos found themselves faced with multiple threats to local prosperity. The most serious of these appeared over the issues of protectionism, falsification, and national taxes. Despite earlier promises from the national government, as of 1890 high protective tariffs for wine had yet to appear. The reaction of free trade defenders to the Baring Crisis not only made the desired increase unlikely but also brought demands that existing tariffs be lowered. They were joined by merchants on the coast who sold imported wine, by legitimate importers, and by the producers of artificial "wine." In the meantime, the rise in shipping costs for both domestic and imported wine as a result of the escalating premium provided fertile ground for the falsification business. Given the nature of the crisis, the national government obviously had severe revenue problems. Higher tariffs could yield more income but so could "temporary" taxes on internal production. Along with several other products, wine looked like a good candidate for such a tax.

All of these problems lay outside the realm of provincial control. The crisis of the 1890s shattered the original supposition of the developmental elite that internal measures alone, assuming the existence of opportunity, would generate economic growth. The awakening they experienced in reaction to the negative aspects of external dependency led to institutionalizing previously used defenses. Private citizens formed voluntary associations with the cooperation and support of the government to defend the province's interests against all of the outside threats. Together, these associations and the government joined in an interprovincial campaign against falsification and internal processing taxes, and for increased protective tariffs. The lobbying effort was strong and largely successful. The revival of the national economy helped in some cases, but pressure had fallen on the national executive from all sides and not all domestic industrialists or internal producers had succeeded.[1]

Cooperation between the government and voluntary associations on economic issues stemmed from Spanish practices in the colonial period. The late Bourbons had worked closely with economic societies in advancing their reforms. In Mendoza, the relatively small number and cohesiveness of the developmental elite obviated the need for such a formal connection between economic interests and public officials, especially since the elite controlled the government until the early 1890s. Still, at least from the beginning of Mendoza's early modern development the province had had one central association that encompassed all commercial and agricultural interests. With the crisis of the 1890s a separate association was created which represented the viticultural sector itself. By this time the political cohesion of the elite had begun to fracture while the number of viticulturalists had expanded greatly and a middle class had begun to emerge. The voluntary associations served to override conflicts imbedded in these changes and to maintain economic cohesion, especially with respect to external forces. [2]

After the turn of the century a new era of accelerated growth occurred for both the nation and the province. Exports rose sharply in the face of expanding markets, unprecedented immigration began, and commerce revived. With protective tariffs for wine assured, national pure wine standards set, and national taxation limited to artificial wine, provincial interests turned their attention to internal matterns of traditional concern: irrigation, education, public interest lobbying, and technical modernization. This last element posed a more serious problem than the developmental elite had anticipated in earlier years.

The voluntary associations which originated in the early 1890s served not only to defend the local economy against the threats of the moment but also to promote modernization and higher quality production. These were traditional concerns of the local elite but their assumption that education and successful examples would lead others to adopt technology and applied science as their guidelines proved erroneous. The rapid expansion of markets left plenty of room for the operations of unscrupulous producers. Local pure wine laws, adopted in the early 1890s, were difficult to enforce. The commercialization of wine was haphazard and largely beyond local control until the turn of the century. By then the combination of various weaknesses in the viticultural sector had given rise to a severe commercial crisis.

The local crisis of 1902-03 came as a delayed effect of the recession of the 1890s. It originated in the particular nature of viticulture. Since vines take several years to mature those planted at the end of the first provincial boom in anticipation of growing demand ended up reaching full bearing when recession reigned. By the beginning of the century with national markets not yet revived, the industry suffered from supplies far in excess of demand. An investigatory commission from the national government used the occasion to chronicle the many difficiencies that existed in the industry. The commission also emphasized the deleterious effects of wine falsification and national taxation. It was obvious that reform was greatly needed. But the pressures from the crisis which might have forced reforms soon dissipated in light of the coastal economy's second boom period.

For several years the provincial and national wine associations continued to propagate technical improvements, better organization for the commercialization of wine, and the need to coordinate grape supplies with bodega capacities and external demand. At the same time, the success of several vintners had resulted in the establishment of a few very large bodegas. This introduced a new complication to the industry in that small producers started selling their wine to large firms for later resale. The large bodegas began to exercise direct control over the commercialization of wine in distant markets. Although only a small percentage of wine was sold between bodegas before 1914 and the control of sales on the coast by large bodegas would not be crucial until after 1914, the early events which led to this began toward the end of Mendoza's second boom.

By 1907 progressive leaders of the industry had formed an association designed to eliminate many of the problems in coordinating local supply and external demand. Despite charges of oligopoly, private efforts continued for several years to create a more comprehensive association that would include both grape and wine producers and that would help eliminate structural problems in the industry while serving as a medium for the dissemination of modern techniques and arbitrating intra-industrial disputes. They achieved their goal in 1911 over the opposition of many producers who complained about the implied restraint of trade and oligopoly. Since the society's membership included a cross section of producers from small to large, and since it also represented most of the producers noted for their progressive attitudes, the opposition probably came from a combination of laissez faire defenders and the less scrupulous industrialists whose practices contributed little to the reputation of Mendoza's wine but who reaped profits from expanding markets. Regardless of the accuracy of the charges or of the origin of the criticism the society either came too late or was insufficiently powerful to prevent another commercial crisis.

Within a year of the society's founding the national economy began to slump badly in response to impending war in Europe. By 1913-14 a second national recession had begun which brought with it effects similar to the crisis of the 1890s. Immigration declined rapidly, foreign investments fell, coastal markets contracted, and domestic commerce slumped. Wine exports from Mendoza fell, and a commercial recession hit the province as stocks of wine greatly surpassed market demand. This time the provincial government intervened by purchasing surpluses. Although both the provincial and national governments undertook investigations of the wine industry, the effects of external dependency had brought an end to the second period of rapid growth for both the nation and the province.

After two periods of accelerated economic growth Mendoza had gained much from a national economic environment conditioned by external dependency. The range of agricultural and livestock products typical of the province's pre-1880 economy remained virtually unchanged by 1914 while production had expanded significantly in almost every case. This was true even for cattle despite the massive increase in stockraising on the pampa. Only wheat production declined in the early twentieth century after having increased in the 1880s and 1890s. Traditional transandine exports had set record highs while imports dropped to negligible levels as eastward commerce escalated. Most eastward exports declined after 1900 as the viticultural industry expanded rapidly. Mendoza's population had tripled with the help of heavy immigration during the second boom and commercial investment had increased markedly. Local taxation of exported wine fed millions of pesos into the provincial treasury, liberating Mendoza from financial dependency (and its political ramifications) on the national government and providing revenue for public sector investments. With less than four percent of the national population, the province held six percent of the country's industrial establishments and eleven percent of all industrial capital. Banking capital had increased fivefold since 1895.

General prosperity rested on the vitality of the viticultural sector and the latter reacted to the way in which coastal markets expanded or contracted as a result of the agro-export sector's external dependence. This statement is made from an interior coastal point of view. Relying on aggregate data at the national level most analysts have made this observation in reverse and taken a coastal-interior orientation. They have focused on the predominance of railroads on the pampa, the nature of the coastal economy, and the singular presence of wine in Mendoza's export accounts (or sugar in Tucumán). Doing so has led them to assign a degree of causality to the coastal-interior linkage that this case study will not support. On a more general level analysts have singled out the lack of social modernization, including appropriate entrepreneurial behavior, as a major contributing factor to the failure of countries like Argentina which have so many other variables in their favor to develop fully. Observers have often pointed to the inhibitory effects of Latin American traditional culture on modernization and development.[3]

The pattern of economic decisionmaking and the fundamental principles at work in the public and private sectors of Mendoza's economy offer a different explanation for many developmental problems. In the nineteenth century the progressive elite followed a pattern of developmental investment both as individuals and as public officials. They invested in infrastructure, emphasized practical education, reinvested their earnings to expand their businesses, and exhibited pride in both initiative and hard work. Carlos Villanueva's condemnation of the lack of initiative and hard work among landholders on the pampa is very telling. In the private sector the progressive mendocinos, joined by immigrants from Spain and Italy, seemed to follow a pattern more typical of a protestant capitalist ethic than of traditional Latin American culture.

On the other hand, the public sector worked closely with private entrepreneurs to intervene directly in the province's growth. Government officials used their power in conjunction with private organizations to defend and advance Mendoza's interests before audiences outside of the province. At times the province offered subsidies to those organizations as well. Although the government quickly reacted to outside threats to the local economy it did little to combat internal threats represented by the severe problems in the wine industry until 1914 when it agreed to purchase surplus stocks. Despite this apparent contradiction, provincial public policy followed a pattern which typified neither the national government nor nineteenth-century liberal capitalism in general. Its actions did parallel a tradition of public policymaking extending back to the late Bourbon period, and in some respects earlier in that century. In fact, the government's failure to intervene in the wine industry may also stem from the same era. The late Bourbons had abandoned direct intervention in the technical side of most industrial operations, preferring to leave those up to private individuals.[4]

If tradition offers an explanation for the basis of public sector decisionmaking it may also contribute to understanding the forces at work in the private sector. It is certainly highly unlikely that the

elite in an area as traditional as Mendoza suddenly took a lesson
from north Atlantic models and adopted the capitalists' ethos. In
any event, they exhibited supposed attributes of that ethos decades
before the advent of nineteenth-century capitalism to Argentina.
Even if they had undergone culture change, their actions as public
officials would then be contradictory to what the change required;
and there is no evidence that the mendocinos suffered from either
culture clash or schizophrenia.

Instead, the explanation for the union of action between the
public and private sectors as well as for the forces at work in the
two arenas seems to stem from an extension of traditional cultural
principles. Under protestant capitalism the anonymous acquisition of
private wealth through hard work and sound investment is its own
reward. In Mendoza, the reward for hard work, sound investment,
and progressive business practices was public recognition which, in
turn, sanctioned the acquisition of wealth.[5] Public rewards were
based on the idea of individual action contributing to the public or
collective welfare. Entrepreneurial behavior or public policies
perceived as detrimental to the common welfare were condemned,
regardless of their profitability for individuals. The community
worked together to advance the interests of all individuals; actions
favoring the few over the many, or one sector over another were
unacceptable. From that, for example, followed the policy of
encouraging small- to medium-scale property holding against the
interests of those who sought extremely large water concessions
without discouraging large-scale agriculture. The public focus of
private action is also exemplified by published statements of the
Centro Vitivinícola in 1910 to the effect that in Mendoza the
emphasis was on one's productivity as a contribution to the
collective wealth of the province and not on the acquisition of empty
titles (law and medicine) representing professions one will never
pursue.

The public orientation of decisionmaking at all levels was
reinforced by values typical of the extended family. From the 1860s
to the 1890s the provincial elite exhibited a strong degree of
cohesion drawn from social and familial ties often reinforced by
marriage patterns. The members of the "provincial family"
reinforced one another's search for individual achievement,
channeled the search along lines of public benefit, and rewarded
success through the assignment of status, prestige, and power.

Vociferous arguments and exaggerated conflict occurred within
the "family" but not as a manifestation of disunity; it represented
instead the expression of individualism within the constraints of
familial devotion and often the need to arrive at decisions of common
benefit. Issues were best left alone if their solutions tended toward
real disunity. Against outside threats the "family" members closed
ranks in a common, almost impregnable defense. Immigrants and the
rising middle class were incorporated into this value system through
the use of voluntary associations. The process was probably
assisted by the fact that so many of the immigrants came from Italy
and Spain; cultures which shared many of these values.

Certain aspects of this cultural foundation to economic
decisionmaking in Mendoza were also at work in other areas. In
Colombia, the early nineteenth-century elite favored technical
education and attempted to channel the young away from traditional
careers in law, politics, and letters toward more productive fields.

The Columbian elite, however, often represented careers and expressed values that were "now" in disfavor and thus served as poor examples. Progressive stockraisers and agriculturalists on the pampa, and supporters of Argentine industrialization in the late nineteenth century likewise exhibited similar values to those at work in Mendoza. In more recent times, one investigation has found that the internal organization of the Argentine industrial giant SIAM, founded by Torcuato DiTella, rested on traditional culture values.[6]

In most instances, the appearance of traditional values supportive of economic growth failed either because they were not adopted by wider segments of the population or because they were not complemented by public policies appropriately derived from the same culture traditions. If Latin American tradition contains regressive quasi-feudal institutions and culture traits inherited from the colonial period and certain aspects of Spanish imperialism it also contains both institutions and traits supportive of growth and development. The latter complex dominated in Mendoza and supported the forces at work and the actions taken within the public and private sectors which played a major role in determining the province's economic success. That the "success" came in the face of frequent threats from the negative impact of external dependency and from the powerful influence of coastal vested interests makes the achievement all the more noteworthy.

A different culture stream with its source in Latin American tradition was at work elsewhere in the country. This was especially true for many of the interior provinces and for a large segment of the traditional landholding elite on the pampa.[7] In some cases Argentine entrepreneurs attempted to adopt an economic ethic characteristic of north Atlantic capitalism and drafted corresponding public policies. But that ethic originated in a different value system based on distinct cultural characteristics and thus ran antithetical to the entrepreneurs' own values. This made the attempt as counterproductive to development as the maintenance of quasi-feudal traditions, while the public policies they formulated inhibited action supportive of development by those entrepreneurs operating within their common basic cultural heritage. The mendocino syndrome suggests strongly that in arenas outside of the value system which gave birth to western capitalism, tradition is at least as crucial to development as sociocultural modernization.

Speculation about such fundamental linkages aside this case study demonstrates that a complicated symbiotic relation existed among the main areas of economic decisionmaking in Mendoza which supported the province's diversified economic growth within an expansionist national economy conditioned by external dependency. To be sure, a single area represented by the federal capital and the province of Buenos Aires consumed the majority of wine exports by the early twentieth century. But behind the export figures stands a simple statistical reality which bears exploration. The percentage distributions of wine exports by province mask both the real increments in traditional markets outside of the littoral and the fact that the province had doubled its provincial markets from seven to fourteen between 1894 and 1911.

In one sense, the almost linear relationship between supply in Mendoza and demand on the coast stemmed from no more sophisticated a variable than that the majority of the population lived in the coastal markets. Given the expansion of Mendoza's markets it is clear that neither the pattern of the railroad networks, nor the structure of the national economy discriminated against the interior trade in wine. Volume was low because the population of consumer markets outside of the littoral was low. Presumably, if more people had lived in the interior, if more migrants had moved to the interior then the volume and the vitality of interregional trade outside of the dynamic core of the national economy would have been far greater.

Obviously, the nature of the agro-export coastal economy and the well-known regressive practices of large landholders on the pampa contributed significantly to the mushrooming population of coastal cities, especially Buenos Aires, during the era of national expansion. But these forces did not prevent immigrants from moving off the coast into the interior. The dynamic economy of Mendoza and the opportunities for personal advancement it offered had attracted tens of thousands of immigrants during the same era in which the coastal population swelled so rapidly. If other interior economies had grown in a fashion similar to that of Mendoza the native and immigrant populations of the interior would have increased accordingly. All other things being equal this would have provided for a better distribution of the national population and, perhaps, the substance on which to build more diversified economies.

This is not to argue that interior development would have overridden coastal growth, but the demographics of Mendoza's wine exports do symbolize larger processes. [8] The economic success or failure of individual provinces may have stemmed more from forces at work within the interior than from the policies of the national government, the structure of the country's transportation system, or the emergence of an externally dependent national agro-export industry. At the very least the lopsided development of Argentina before World War I, as well as the center-periphery and dependency structures contemporary scholars have described, have a distinct image when viewed from the interior.

Endnotes for Chapter 5

1. For a summary analysis of the protectionist battle see Donna J. Guy, "Carlos Pellegrini and the Politics of Early Argentine Industrialization, 1873-1906," *Journal of Latin American Studies*, 2,1 (May 1979): 123-44.

2. A similar argument is advanced by Jorge Balan in his "Una cuestión regional en la Argentina: Burguesías provinciales y el mercado nacional en el Desarrollo agroexportador," *Desarrollo Económico*, 18, 69 (April-June 1978): 49-87.

3. The analysis in this section on values, culture, entrepreneurship, and development is based on a wide variety of sources. The most often cited critic of Argentine culture in this context is Tomás Fillol, *Social Factors in Economic Development: The Argentine Case* (Cambridge, Massachusetts, 1961). Modern observers have discredited such culturally biased arguments within the contemporary scene. See, for example, Guillermo Edelberg, "Managerial Resource Development in Argentina," in *Latin American Management: Development and Performance*, ed. Robert R. Rehdler (Reading, Massachusetts, 1968). Also see Fleming, "The Cultural Determinants of Entrepreneurship and Economic Development: A Case Study of Mendoza, Argentina, 1861-1914," *Journal of Economic History*, 39, 1 (March 1979): 211-24.

    An excellent bibliographical review is Nathaniel H. Leff, "Entrepreneurship and Economic Development: The Problem Revisited," *Journal of Economic Literature*, 17, 1 (March 1979): 46-64.

4. See the sections on public policy and economic growth in the late eighteenth century in: Manuel Comeiro, *Historia de la economía política en España*, 2 vols. (Madrid, Spain 1965); Antonio Domínguez Ortiz, et al., *Los borbones: El siglo XVIII en España y América*, vol. 4 of *Historia de España y América: Social y económica*, edited by Jaime Vicens Vives (Barcelona, Spain 1972); and Richard Herr, *The Eighteenth-Century Revolution in Spain* (Princeton, New Jersey 1969). The relationship between educational reform and political economy is discussed briefly in various parts of Richard Kagen, *Students and Society In Early Modern Spain* (Baltimore, Maryland 1974). The effect of the reforms on Colombia's early modern political economy is addressed by Frank Safford, *The Ideal of the Practical: Colombia's Struggle To Form a Technical Elite* (Austin, Texas 1976). See also Ann Twinam, *Miners, Merchants, and Farmers in Colonial Colombia* (Austin, Texas 1982).

5. Although I had been grappling toward this notion for some time, my ideas congealed only after reading Glenn Dealy's imaginative and well-reasoned study, *The Public Man: An Interpretation of Latin America and Other Catholic Countries* (Amherst, Massachusetts 1977).

6. Thomas Cochran and Ruben Reina, *Entrepreneurship in Argentine Culture: Tocuato Di Tella and S.I.A.M.* (Philadelphia, Pennsylvania 1962).

7. On the interior see, for example, Donna J. Guy, *Argentine Sugar Politics: Tucumán and the Generation of Eighty* (Tempe, Arizona 1980), and Scott Whiteford, *Workers From The North: Plantations, Bolivian Labor, and the City in Northwest Argentina* (Austin, Texas 1981).

8. Jonathan C. Brown assigns a crucial role to interior commerce in stimulating early nineteenth-century interest in Buenos Aires as a port and similarly qualifies the adverse effects of Buenos Aires' subsequent rapid growth on the interior. See his, *A Socioeconomic History of Argentina, 1776–1860* (New York, New York 1979), especially pp. 72 and 202.

BIBLIOGRAPHY

Periodicals Consulted

Economist, The (London), 1880-1914.

El Economista Argentino (Buenos Aires), 1893-94.

La Viticultura Argentina (Buenos Aires), 1911.

Los Andes (Mendoza), 1882-1914

Review of the River Plate, The (Buenos Aires), 1891-1914.

Official Publications

Album Argentino. Provincia de Mendoza, su vida, su trabajo, su progreso. (Buenos Aires) 1910.

Album de Mendoza mandado publicar por S. E. el Gobernador . . . con motivo de la Exposición Industrial del Centenario. (Mendoza: n.p.) 1910.

Alcorta, Santiago, ed. *La República Argentina en la Exposición Universal de París de 1889.* 2 vols. (Paris: Sociedad Anónima de Publicacciones Periódicas) 1890.

Alurralde, Carlos. *Memoria presentada a la Comisión Central de Extinción de la Langosta.* (Mendoza: Tipografía Los Andes) 1898.

Anales de Agricultura, 1873-1876. (Buenos Aires: Departamento Nacional de Agricultura).

Anuario de la Dirección General de Estadística (Mendoza) 1881-87, 1903, 1906-14. Title varies. Suspended publication 1888-1902, 1904-05, although the volume for 1906 contains data from 1904 and 1905.

Arata, Pedro N., et al. *Investigación vinícola complementaria de 1904.* (Buenos Aires: Imprenta de M. Biedma e Hijo) 1904.

_____. *Investigación vinícola: Informes* (Buenos Aires: Talleres de Publicaciones de la Oficina Meteorológica Argentina) 1903.

Boletín del Ministerio de Obras Públicas (Buenos Aires) 1901-02, 1911-14. Suspended publication 1901-10.

Boletín del Ministerio de Agricultura (Buenos Aires) 1878-97, 1901-03, 1905-14. Title varies.

Censo Agropecuario Nacional (Buenos Aires) 1937.

Censo General de la Provincia (Mendoza) 1909. The only provincial census taken between 1864 and 1914.

Censo Nacional de 1869 (Buenos Aires) 1872.

Censo Nacional de 1895, 3 vols. (Buenos Aires) 1898.

Censo Nacional de 1914, 10 vols. (Buenos Aires) 1916-17.

Diario de Sesiones de la Cámara de Diputados (National) 1862-86.

Diario de Sesiones de la Cámara de Senadores (National), 1862-1914.

Díaz Guzmán, José M. Indice General de leyes de la Provincia, 1896-1914 (Mendoza: Talleres Gráficos D'Accurzio) 1849.

Digesto del Departamento General de Irrigación (Mendoza). (Mendoza: Casa Jacobo Peuser) 1929.

Dirección General de Comercio. Censo industrial y comercial de la República Argentina, 1904-14. (Buenos Aires: Talleres Gráficos del Ministerio de Agricultura) 1915. A compilation of 20 "bulletins."

Discurso del Gobernador de la Provincia de Mendoza D. Tiburcio Benegas al recibirse del mando el 15 de febrero de 1887. (Mendoza: Tipografía "Bazar Madrileño") 1887.

El Comercio Exterior Argentino (Buenos Aires) 1882-1914; preceded by Estadística de las Aduanas de la República Argentina (Buenos Aires) 1870-81; preceded by Registro Estadístico de la República Argentina (Buenos Aires) 1864-69.

Informe del Departamento de Agricultura (Buenos Aires) 1872-73.

Junta Reguladora de Vinos. Recopilación de leyes, decretos, disposiciones sobre la industria vitivinícola. 2 vols. (Buenos Aires: Guillermo Kraft) 1938.

Lahitte, Emilio, ed. Informe y estudios de la Dirección de Economía Rural y Estadística. 3 vols. (Buenos Aires: Talleres Gráficos del Ministerio de Agricultura de la Nación) 1916.

Lahitte, Emilio. "Boletín de estadística agrícola del año 1905." Boletín del Ministerio de Agricultura (Buenos Aires) 1906 5:57-70.

Lemos, Abraham. Memoria descriptiva de la Provincia: Obra mandada ejecutar por el Exmo. Gobierno de la Provincia para concurrir a la Exposición de París en 1889. (Mendoza: Tipografía y Papelería "Los Andes") 1888.

Memoria del Ministerio de Agricultura (Buenos Aires) 1873-1910, 1912-14. Title varies.

Memoria del Ministro de Hacienda. (Mendoza) 1888, 1898-99, 1911. Publisher and title varies.

Memoria del año . . . presentada al la honorable Legislatura por el Ministro de Gobierno y Hacienda. (Mendoza) 1879, 1880. Publisher varies.

Memoria del Segundo Congreso de Comercio e Industrias. (Mendoza) 1914.

Mensaje del Gobernador de la Provincia al abrir el primer periodo de sessiones el 3 de febrero de 1880. (Mendoza: Imprenta de "El Constitucional") 1880. With variations in title and publisher these published versions of the provincial governors' messages are available for various sessions of the provincial legislature between 1884 and 1906.

Ministerio del Interior. Departamento General de Irrigación. *La Provincia de Mendoza: su producción vitícola, agrícola, minera y ganadera.* (Buenos Aires, n.p.) 1893?

Primer Censo Municipal de Población. (Mendoza City) 1903.

Pavlowsky, Aaron. *Informe presentado al Exmo. Sr. Ministro del Interior. . . sobre los trabajos ejecutados en la Escuela Nacional de Agricultura de Mendoza en el ano de 1884.* (Mendoza: Imprenta de La Palabra) 1885.

Recopilación de leyes desde el primero de enero de 1896 al 31 de diciembre de 1924. (Mendoza) To be used with Díaz Guzmán cited above.

Registro Oficial de Mendoza. (Mendoza) 1869-1914.

Síntesis de los anuarios de la Dirección General de Estadística, 1915-1922 (Mendoza). (Buenos Aires: Talleres Casa Jacobo Peuser) 1923.

Books and Articles

Alberdi, Juan B. *Bases y puntos de partida para la organización política de la República Argentina.* 5th ed. Buenos Aires: n.p., 1933.

Aparicio, Francisco de, and Horacio A. Difieri, eds. *La Argentina: Suma de geografía.* 9 vols. Buenos Aires: n.p., 1958-63.

Araoz, Ernesto M. "Mendoza y Salta a traves de la historia." *Revista de la Junta de Estudios Históricos de Mendoza,* 2:6 (1970): 72-83.

Balán, Jorge. "Una cuestión regional en la Argentina: Burguesías provinciales y el mercado nacional en el desarrollo agroexportador," *Desarrollo Económico,* 18:69 (1978): 49-87.

_____, and Nancy Lopez, "Burguesías y gobiernos en la Argentina: La política impositiva de Tucumán y Mendoza entre 1873 y 1914," *Desarrollo Económico,* 17:67 (October-December, 1977), chart 4.

Balbín, Valentín. *Sistema de medidas y pesas de la República Argentina.* Buenos Aires: Tipografía de M. Biedma, 1881.

Bergquist, Charles. "On Paradigms and the Pursuit of the Practical," *Latin American Research Review,* 13:2 (1978): 247-51.

Best, Felix y Luis Castro Bustos, eds. *Gufa Comercial e Industrial de Mendoza,* 1903, 1908.

Best, Felix, ed. *Gufa Best: Gufa de las provincias de Mendoza, San Juan y San Luis.* Imprenta "La Perseverancia," 1904.

Blanco, Eusebio. "Las viñas y los vinos en Mendoza." *Boletín del Departamento Nacional de Agricultura* (Buenos Aires) part 1, 8 (1884): 213-26; part 2, 8 (1884): 253-72.

Bueri, Lelia I. *Catálogo de estadísticas publicadas en la República Argentina.* 2 vols. Buenos Aires: Editorial del Instituto Torcuato Di Tella, 1963.

Brown, Jonathan C. *A Socioeconomic History of Argentina, 1776-1860.* Cambridge, England: Cambridge University Press, 1979.

Burmeister, Hermann. *Viaje por los estados del Plata.* Buenos Aires, 1943.

Caballero, Claudio. "Exposición de Mendoza: Escuela Nacional de Agricultura." *Boletín del Departamento Nacional de Agricultura,* 7 (15 June 1883): 338-44.

_____. "Exposición de Mendoza: Productos Agrícolas." *Boletín del Departamento Nacional de Agricultura,* 7 (30 June 1883): 353-68.

Campoy, Luis. "Persistencia de algunas valores sociales en una sociedad en desarrollo." *Investigaciones en Sociología,* 4 (1965): 53-84.

Cano, Guillerno J. *Régimen jurídico económico de las aguas en Mendoza (1810-1884).* Mendoza: Librería de la Universidad, 1941.

Carosso, Vincent P. *The California Wine Industry: A Study of the Formative Years.* Berkeley: University of California Press, 1951.

Casares, Cesar. "Informe sobre el mercado de la provincia de Mendoza." *Boletín del Ministerio de Agricultura,* 14 (January 1912): 3-17.

Castro Bustos, Luis. *Justo Castro, gobernador de San Juan y su influencia en el desarrollo de la industria vitivinícola del pais.* Buenos Aires: Talleres Gráficos Argentinos, 1939.

Centro Comercial, Agrícola e Industrial. *Memoria descriptiva y estadística de la provincia de Mendoza.* Mendoza: Tipografía "La Perserverancia," 1893.

Centro Comercial, Agrícola e Industrial. *Solicitud que los bodegueros y viñateros de la Provincia de Mendoza elevan al Honorable Congreso de la Nación, pidiendo la no aceptación del impuesto de 2 centavos por cada litro de vino nacional.* Mendoza, n.p., 1897.

Centro Comercial, Agrícola y Industrial. *Exposición presentada a los Señores Diputados y Senadores al H. Congreso Nacional sobre la importancia de la industria vitivinícola.* Mendoza: Tipografía "Los Andes," 1894.

Centro Vitivinícola Argentino. *Petición al Honorable Congreso de la Nación con motivo del proyecto de Ley de Aduanas.* Buenos Aires: ARGOS, 1895.

Centro Vitivinícola Argentino. *Petición al H. Congreso de la Nación: Modificaciones de la Ley de Impuestos Internos.* Buenos Aires: Talleres Gráficos de "El Correo Español," 1896.

Centro Vitivinícola Nacional. *La Vitivinicultura Argentina en 1910.* Buenos Aires, 1910.

Centro de Almaceneros. *La nueva Ley de Vinos: Solicitudes presentadas por . . . a los poderes públicos pidiendo su derogación o reforma.* Buenos Aires: Tipo-Lito "Galileo," 1905.

Chapman, Charles E. *A History of Spain.* New York: Macmillan, 1918.

Civit, Emilio. *Los viñedos de Francia y los de Mendoza: Importante carta del Dr. Emilio Civit al Sr. Tiburcio Benegas.* Mendoza: Tipografía Los Andes, 1887.

Coni, Emilio R. *Sanaemiento de la Provincia de Mendoza.* Buenos Aires: Imprenta de Pablo E. Coni e Hijos, 1897.

Correas, Edmundo. "Doctor Exequiel Tabanera (1830-1912)." *Revista de la Junta de Estudios Históricos de Mendoza,* 2:7 (1972): 59-76.

Crawford, Robert. *Across the Pampas and the Andes.* London: Longmans, Green, and Company, 1884.

Cutolo, Vicente Osvaldo, ed. *Nuevo diccionario biográfico argentino (1750-1930).* 3 vols. Buenos Aires: Editorial ELCHE, 1969.

De Vries, Egbert de and José M. Echavarría, eds. *Social Aspects of Economic Development in Latin America.* 2 vols. UNESCO Technology and Society Series. Tournai, Belgium, 1963.

Denis, Paul Ives. "San Rafael: La ciudad y su region." *Boletín de Estudios Geográficos* (Mendoza), 16 (1969): 131-430.

Diaz Araujo, Enrique. "La explotación de petroleo en Mendoza en el siglo XIX." *Revista de la Junta de Estudios Históricos de Mendoza,* 2:5 (1968): 121-54.

Dorfman, Adolfo. *Historia de la industria argentina.* Buenos Aires: Solar Hachette, 1970.

Dos Santos, Theotonio. "The Structure of Dependence," *American Economic Review,* 60:2 (1970): 232.

Fernández, Mirta, et al. "Mendoza y el litoral al comenzar la Guerra del Paraguay." *Revista de la Junta de Estudios Históricos de Mendoza,* 2:7 (1972): 669-84.

Ferns, Henry S. *Britain and Argentina in the Nineteenth Century.* Oxford: Clarendon Press, 1960.

Ferraro, Roque M. *El desarrollo regional argentino: problemática y posibilidades.* Buenos Aires: Editorial Plus Ultra, 1973.

Ferrer, Aldo. *La economía argentina: Las etapas de su desarrollo y problemas actuales.* Buenos Aires: Talleres Gráficos de la Compañía Impresora Argentina, 1971.

Ford, A.G. *The Gold Standard 1880-1914: Britain and Argentina.* New York: Oxford University Press, 1962.

Fraboschi, Roberto O. "Historia de la agricultura, la ganadería y la industria." In *La Argentina: Suma de geografía,* vol. 4, edited by Francisco de Aparicio and Horacio A. Difieri, pp. 159-260. Buenos Aires: Ediciones Peuser, 1959.

Fraser, John F. *The Amazing Argentine: A New Land of Enterprise.* New York: Funk and Wagnalls, 1914.

Funes, Lucio. *Gobernadores de Mendoza.* 2 vols. Mendoza: Best Hnos., 1942, 1951.

Galanti, A.N. *La industria viti-vinícola argentina.* 2 vols. Buenos Aires: Talleres S. Ostwald y Cía., 1900.

Galdames, Luis. *A History of Chile.* Chapel Hill, N.C.: University of North Carolina Press, 1948.

Gallo, Ezequiel. *Farmers in Revolt.* London: The Athlone Press, 1976.

Gallo, Ezequiel, and Roberto Cortés Conde. *Argentina: La República Conservadora. Historia Argentina,* vol. 5. Buenos Aires: Editorial Paidos, 1972.

García, Agustín. *La irrigación en la Provincia de Mendoza.* 2d ed. Mendoza: Tip. "La Perseverancia," 1902.

Goldsmith, Peter H. *Argentina.* New York: Inter-American Press, 1924.

Guy, Donna J. *Argentine Sugar Politics: Tucumán and the Generation of Eighty.* Tempe, Arizona, 1980.

_____. "Carlos Pelligrini and the Politics of Early Argentine Industrialization, 1873-1906," *Journal of Latin American Studies,* 2:1 (1979): 123-44.

Hirschman, Albert O. *The Strategy of Economic Development.* New Haven: Yale University Press, 1958.

Kagan, Richard. *Students and Society in Early Modern Spain.* Baltimore, 1974.

"La industria vinícola." *El Economista Argentina,* 2:99 (21 October 1893): 4-5.

"La unión gremial entre viñateros y bodegueros de Mendoza." *La Viticultura Argentina,* 2 (1911): 153-70.

Latzina, Francisco. *Estadística retrospectivo del comercio exterior argentino, 1875-1904.* Buenos Aires: Compañía Sud-America de Billetes de Banco, 1905.

_____. *Geografía de la República Argentina.* Buenos Aires: Felix Lajouane, 1888.

_____. *L'Agriculture et l'elevage dans le Republique Argentine.* Buenos Aires: n.p., 1888.

Lipset, Seymour Martin and Aldo Solari, eds. *Elites in Latin America.* New York, 1967.

Llerena, Juan. "Cuadros descriptivos estadísticos de las tres provincias de Cuyo." *Revista de Buenos Aires,* 9 (1866): 105-12, 273-88, 389-421, 576-89; 10 (1866): 89-108, 263-301, 398-408, 572-92; 11 (1866): 62-79, 280-95.

Los Argentinos a S.A.R. El Príncipe Di Piemonte Umberto Di Savola en ocasión de su visita a Mendoza. (photo album) Buenos Aires: Talleres Gráficos de la Compañía General de Fósforos, 1927.

Love, Joseph L. "Raul Prebisch and the Origins of the Doctrine of Unequal Exchange," *Latin American Research Review,* 15:3 (1980): 45-72.

Martin de Moussy, and Jean Antoine Victor. *Description géographique et statistique de la Conféderation Argentine.* Paris: Librairie de Firmin Didot Freres, Fils et Cie., 1860-64.

Martínez, Alberto B., and Maurice Lewandowski. *The Argentine in the Twentieth Century.* London: T. Fisher Unwine, 1911.

Martínez, Pedro Santos, ed. *Contribuciones para la historia de Mendoza.* Mendoza: Universidad Nacional de Cuyo, 1969.

_____. "La irrigación de Mendoza durante el virreinato (1776-1810)." *Revista de la Junta de Estudios Históricos de Mendoza,* 2:1 (1961): 41-68.

_____. "Mendoza, 1862-1892: Ensayo de interpretación sociopolítico." In *Contribución para la historia de Mendoza,* edited by Pedro Santos Martínez, pp. 131-78. Mendoza: Universidad Nacional de Cuyo, 1969.

_____. *Historia económica de Mendoza durante el virreinato, 1776-1810.* Madrid: Gráficos ORBE, 1961.

Masini Calderón, José Luis. *Mendoza hace cien años: historia de la provincia durante la presidencia de Mitre.* Buenos Aires: Ediciones Theoria, 1967.

Maurín Navarro, Emilio. *Contribución al estudio de la historia vitivinícola argentina: Producción, comercio e indústrias de San Juan desde su fundación hasta comienzos del siglo XX.* Mendoza: Imprenta López, 1967.

Molins, W. Jaime, and Jorge Dantil, eds. *La República Argentina: Región de Cuyo: San Juan, Mendoza, San Luis.* Buenos Aires: Talleres Gráficos "Oceana," 1922?

Morales Guiñazú, Fernando. *Historia de la cultura mendocina.* Biblioteca de la Junta de Estudios Históricos de Mendoza. vol. 4. Mendoza: Best Hermanos, 1943.

Mulhall, Michael G. *Handbook of the River Plate.* London: K. Paul, Trench Co., 1892.

Mulhall, Michael G., and Edward T. Mulhall. *Handbook of the River Plate Republics.* London: William Clowes and Sons, 1875.

Museo de Productos Argentinos. *Primer Catálogo.* Buenos Aires, n.p., 1889.

Newton, Jorge. *Diccionario biográfico del campo argentino.* Buenos Aires, 1972.

Ortíz, Ricardo M. *Historia económica de la Argentina.* Buenos Aires: Plus Ultra, 1971.

Pacottet, Pablo. *Vinificación en la Provincia de Mendoza.* París: Librería J. B. Bailliere e Hijo, 1911.

Palencia, Richard. "The Wine-Growing Industry In The Argentine Republic." *Agricultural and Pastoral Census of the Nation,* vol. 3. Buenos Aires: Printing Works of the Argentine Meteorological Office, pp. 253-63.

Pavlowsky, Aaron. *La industria viti-vinícola nacional.* Buenos Aires: Imprenta de Pablo E. Coni e Hijos, 1894.

_____. *La viticultura en la República Argentina: Conferencia dada durante la Exposición-Feria en Mercedes (Buenos Aires) en 18 y el 19 de septiembre de 1887.* Mendoza: Tip. a vapor "Bazar Madrileño," 1888.

_____. *Conferencia sobre viticultura.* San Juan: Tip. de la Unión, 1885.

_____. *Informe presentado al Exmo. Sr. Ministro del Interior Dr. D. Bernardo de Irigoyén sobre los trabajos ejecutados en la Escuela Nacional de Agricultura de Mendoza en el año de 1884.* Mendoza: Imprenta de La Palabra, 1885.

Peck, Donald. "Argentinian Politics and the Province of Mendoza, 1890-1916." unpublished Ph.D. thesis. Oxford University, 1977.

Pérez, Flavio, ed. *Guía de Mendoza.* Mendoza, 1888, 1895, 1897-98, 1901.

Platt, D.C.M. "Dependency in Nineteenth-Century Latin America: An Historian Objects," *Latin American Research Review,* 15:1 (1980): 113-30.

Queyrat, Enrique. *Los buenos vinos argentinos.* Buenos Aires, Libreria Hachette, 1974.

Rickard, F. Ignacio. *A Mining Journey Across the Great Andes: With Explorations in the Silver Mining Districts of the Provinces of San Juan and Mendoza, and a Journey Across the Pampas to Buenos Aires.* London: Smith, Elder Co. , 1863.

Rock, David. *Politics in Argentina, 1890-1930.* London: Cambridge University Press, 1975.

Rodríguez Añido, Federico. "La cuestión de los vinos y los viti-vinicultores argentinos." *El Economista Argentina,* 154 (1894):3.

_____. "Proteccionismo y libre-cambio: Los vinos, los azúcares, los tabacos." *El Economista Argentina,* 143 (1894): 3-4.

Rodríguez, Luis D. *La Argentina en 1912.* Buenos Aires: Compañía Sud-Americana de Billetes de Banco, 1912.

_____. *La Argentina: Descripción de la Capital Federal, provincias y territorios naciones. Estadística comercial. Productos. Industrias en explotación. Valor de los terrenos de cultivos y destinados a la ganadería en la República, basado en las últimas ventas.* Buenos Aires: Companía Sud-America de Billetes de Banco, 1908.

Romano, Aníbal Mario. "El terremoto de 1861." In *Repercusiones de Pavón en Mendoza a través del periodismo, 1861-1863,* edited by Pedro Santos Martínez, pp. 35-82. Mendoza: Universidad Nacional de Cuyo, 1973.

Sabella, Pedro F. *Tratado de geografía general, humana, económica y corográfica de la Provincia de Mendoza.* Mendoza: Imprenta Oficial Escuela de Artes Gráficas para Penados, 1936.

Safford, Frank. "On Paradigms and the Pursuit of the Practical: A Response," *Latin American Research Review,* 13:2 (1978): 252-60.

_____. *The Ideal of the Practical: Colombia's Struggle to Form a Technical Elite.* Austin: University of Texas Press, 1976.

Salviolo Hermanos. *Gran Guía de Cuyo.* 1st ed. Mendoza: Imprenta, Librería, y Encuadernación "Nacional," 1912.

Scalvini, Jorge M. *Historia de Mendoza.* Mendoza, 1965.

Scobie, James R. *Argentina: A City and a Nation.* 2d ed. New York: Oxford University Press, 1971.

_____. *Buenos Aires: Plaza to Suburb, 1870-1910.* New York: Oxford University Press, 1974.

_____. *Revolution on the Pampa: A Social History of Argentine Wheat, 1860-1910.* 2d ed. Austin: University of Texas Press, 1967.

Sergi, Jorge F. *Historia de los italianos en la Argentina.* Buenos Aires: Editorial Italo Argentina, 1940.

Sociedad Union Viti-Vinícola Argentina. *La viña: sus productos e influencia colonizadora, terrenos propios para la plantación de viña, bodegas, personal.* Buenos Aires: Imprenta y Esterotipa del "Courrier de la Plata," 1888.

Stein, Stanley J. and Barbara H. "D.C.M. Platt: The Anatomy of 'Autonomy,'" *Latin American Research Review,* 15:1 (1980): 131-46.

Suárez, Leopoldo. *Experimentos sobre vinificación.* Buenos Aires: Talleres de Publicaciones de la oficina Meteorológica Argentina, 1907.

Tristany, Miguel R. *Guía estadística de la provincia de Mendoza.* Mendoza: Imprenta del Constitucional, 1860.

Vázquez de la Morena, M. "Exposición interprovincial en Mendoza." *Boletín del Departamento Nacional de Agricultura,* 8 (31 October 1884): 667-72.

Vicens Vives, Jaime. *Approaches to the History of Spain.* Berkeley, 1967.

Vicuña MacKenna, Benjamín. *La Argentina en el año 1855.* Buenos Aires: Talleres Gráficos de A. García y Cía., 1936.

Villanueva, Carlos E. *El litoral y el interior: observaciones sobre ganadería y agricultura.* Buenos Aires: Tip., Lit. y Enc. del Colegio Pio IX de Artes y Oficios, 1887.

Villanueva, Joaquín. "Regadío en Mendoza." *Boletín del Departamento Nacional de Agricultura,* 7 (31 January 1883): 59-60.

Williams, John H. *Argentine Trade Under Inconvertible Paper Money, 1880-1900.* Harvard Economic Studies, vol. 22. Cambridge, Massachusetts: Harvard University Press, 1920.